HEALING
Troubled
Relationships

HEALING
Troubled
Relationships

VICTOR L. BROWN, JR.

Bookcraft

Salt Lake City, Utah

Library of Congress Catalog Card Number: 89–83390

ISBN 0–88494–709–2

First Printing, 1989

Printed in the United States of America

those things that please him." (John 8:28–29.) His truths, which are his Father's truths, are confirmed by the Holy Ghost: "I will pray the Father, and he shall give you another Comforter, that he may abide with you for ever; even the Spirit of truth" (John 14:16–17).

The earnest disciple of Christ, then, has the Father, the Son, and the Holy Ghost to guide him in the personal search for truth in relationships. This might be kept in mind whenever this book makes reference to the Savior's teachings, doctrines, and covenants.

Summary

By taking the time and making the effort to gather information and organize our relationship efforts we markedly improve our likelihood of success. Otherwise we will continue to rely on chance rather than take specific steps that produce results.

The pages that follow contain reports of relationships that have been entered into, enriched, or healed. These efforts and their elements, with supporting commentary and evidence, are divided into the three phases of self-definition, self-discipline, and self-understanding.

Self-definition is the conscious effort a person makes to decide who he or she wants to be. It encompasses the work necessary to gain control over our attitudes and behavior—that is, *self-discipline*. Out of these efforts evolves *self-understanding*, a knowledge of who we are and why we behave as we do. These three phases and the steps within them are the framework of our discussion on human relationships.

As we here journey along together, although I will attempt to present organized, methodical ways to begin or maintain or heal relationships, keep in mind the wondrously varied and even exhilarating seasons of human relationships. For every individual and in every significant relationship there are seasons. Spring promises beginnings. Summer can either ripen or scorch. Autumn may bring bounteous harvest or barrenness. Winter's chill causes what was once vibrant to flicker low, even to die. But once again spring appears, which gives us hope. Surely you have seen all these seasons in human relationships. If not, you will, before we are through, for even in the winter of a dead relationship there is the promise of spring and of new life. One social scientist discovered this in an unscientific but nevertheless compelling way:

> Maybe it's my Minnesota upbringing. You have to keep looking, and listening, to see your way through six months of winter, to hear echoes of springtime when the earth is buried beneath three feet of snow and all 10,000 lakes are locked in icy silence . . . cold without end.
>
> The psyche has seasons of its own, and when my marriage plans blew up at the last minute in faith-shaking fashion winter fell in mid-May. I went for a walk, scarcely noticing where I was going, and found myself . . . in an unfamiliar neighborhood. From the open window of a nearby apartment . . . a woman's voice suddenly rang out . . . resonant with gladness, saying, "Hallelujah, thank you, thank you, thank you, hallelujah, thank you," over and over again.
>
> I have no idea what she was grateful for, with what manner of miracle she'd been graced. But her hallelujahs filled the air and warmed it, like a January, . . . thaw bearing promises of new life. I stood rooted to the sidewalk, soaking in the sound even after she had stopped. . . . I walked home with more direction. No matter that it was someone else's miracle, . . . I, too, had received a gift, an offering of hope. (Carol Howard, "Minor Miracles," *Psychology Today,* August 1986, pp. 18, 22. Reprinted with permission from Psychology Today Magazine. Copyright © 1986 [PT Partners, L.P.].)

Self-definition, self-discipline, and self-understanding are never finished conditions. They are journeys through many seasons. Their seekers are perpetual students who cast wary eyes on those who presume to have final answers to every one of life's questions, yet they accept those few absolutes that answer life's crucial questions. They seek wisdom and truth from history, religion, science, and from other human beings. They trust! They risk! They hope!

To Mareen

Contents

Acknowledgments

Church and professional service have allowed me to meet many people who have struggled with life's severest challenges. To them I express gratitude for permitting me to share in their earnest, even noble, efforts to act decently even as they strove to enrich or heal relationships as taught by the Savior.

The creation of a book is a most collaborative project. Over several years, Cory Maxwell of Bookcraft kindly encouraged me to persevere.

Any writer is doomed without a sensitive and skilled editor. George Bickerstaff performed this invaluable labor over the manuscript right up to the final hour.

As this project drew near completion both the content and events caused me to appreciate more than ever, especially as age now takes its relentless toll, the influence of my parents, for their relationship of integrity and love.

Our children and grandchildren in their triumphs and trials provide opportunities to plumb the breadth and depth of love which puts eternal relationships into perspective.

My friend and eternal companion, Mareen, typed, counseled, exemplified, and urged this undertaking to completion. The book, and any good it might promote, is dedicated to her.

I have heard thy prayer,
I have seen thy tears:
behold, I will heal thee.
— 2 Kings 20:5

Enriching and Healing Relationships

CHAPTER ONE

Just two days earlier we had had the best marriage counseling session yet for Clifford* and Marie, but today Clifford was anxiously waiting when I arrived at the office. As soon as we sat down, Clifford began to tell of the argument he and his wife had the previous evening. It seemed that as soon as he had walked through the door after work, Marie attacked him — verbally, fortunately. He was stunned, since she had been so pleasant in the morning as he left for work. I was mystified too, so we arranged for an interview that afternoon.

As it turned out, Marie had in fact bade Clifford a loving goodbye in the morning. During the day, however, while she worked in the kitchen making bread (her husband's favorite treat was jam

---

*Names and identifying information have been changed throughout this book.

and hot homemade bread) there came into her mind a recollection of an unpleasant episode with Clifford twenty-five years earlier at a church social. With increasing emotion Marie mentally replayed and reacted anew to her husband's immature behavior of a quarter century ago. By the time the scoundrel walked through the door that afternoon both she and the bread were hot, and consequently he experienced a different homecoming than the aroma of the fresh bread had set him up to expect. The only positive note about what happened thereafter was that Clifford was too shocked to retaliate.

As Marie and Clifford examined this remarkable episode in my office that afternoon they saw the humor in it. They also saw the lesson it highlighted, for it was symptomatic of their major problem: each expected the other to make their relationship a happy one, so neither partner was taking personal responsibility for the quality of the relationship. Marie and Clifford were bright and effective people. In fact, their friends would have been surprised to know they were seeing a counselor. But they were in serious marital trouble, which was brought about primarily by their incorrect or unrealistic expectations about their relationship. The sad thing was that the relationship need never have deteriorated as it had, that most of their problems could have been prevented. Had they known what to expect of themselves, their relationship would by now have been strong. But in their hunger for the other person to speak, touch, and give reassuring warmth, and in their frustration at not receiving it, each had temporarily lost the ability or the desire to give those very things to the relationship.

These two decent folks are not alone. In our day many people have chosen to modify, repeal, or ignore time-tested values, tried and true rules, about relationships. Lacking those firm standards, they do not know what to expect from themselves or contribute to the relationship. And to complicate matters, they seek to measure the strength of relationships by what they get rather than by what they give, by superficial emotions and ego gratification rather than by deep, rich personal investment. They will not *work* to heal the troubled relationship or to enrich it.

To be human is to need kindness, civility, warmth, affection, and intimacy. All of us yearn for these responses. Yet to our grave harm these essential elements of relationships appear to be evaporating in today's climate of irresponsible and unsubstantiated beliefs about human relationships. Whereas for most of human history laws and customs have reinforced and encouraged relationships, today, especially in the Western world, many laws and customs undermine and even discourage them. From rules of etiquette to powerful norms governing marriage, family, and sexuality, proper attitudes and behaviors have been abandoned at the cost of honorable and enduring human relationships.

On the day this chapter is being written, Sweden has moved to legitimize "marriages" between members of the same sexual gender. Such an effort to formalize and validate homosexual relationships bespeaks deadly disregard for millennia of basic, proven values relating to human relationships. It is true that, for those who can accept homosexual practices as a "different life-style," the granting of legal status for purposes of sex acts and property rights may have some cold logic behind it. But it is a squalid enterprise that seeks to equate either homosexual "marriage" or heterosexual unmarried cohabitation with the institution of traditional marriage —with such values as the family, procreation, nurturance, relationships of extended families across generations. Short-sighted intellectual exercises, social research without regard to historical experience and values, religious beliefs that shift with the tides of political pressures, or just sincere wishing—these do not protect people from the consequences of attitudes and behaviors that harm relationships.

Just as surely, there are attitudes and behaviors that create good relationships or enrich existing ones; or, when needed, heal troubled ones. Clifford and Marie's relationship deteriorated because they lost track of what enriches a relationship. In the beginning each tried to do his or her best, but gradually each came to expect the other person to make the relationship good, and that led to their becoming mired in mutual recrimination —a natural result of such behavior. On the other hand, when someone stops waiting for the other person to love and instead gives love, usually the result is an enriched relationship.

Ask yourself how many people you know who are divorced or are children of divorced parents. Does it seem that in recent years you have met quite a few people who were abused as children? Can you identify men and women who are homosexual? How many single parent households are you aware of? How many latchkey children do you know? Can you name at least one unwed parent? Whom do you know who has chosen not to marry? Why are there so many young adult men who lack the confidence or social skills to court the young women? Whom do you know who is married but is miserable, trapped in an emotional prison? Where has the nuclear family gone? the extended family? Are you a wife and mother who strongly believes in being a homemaker but who feels devalued even by other women? As a husband and father do you wonder just what is expected of you these days?

Does the prevalence of such problems and situations mean that human society is falling apart? There certainly is considerable evidence that, at the very least, dramatic, destructive upheavals are occurring in the area of relationships—unless divorce, sexual chaos, abuse within families, unkindness, and selfishness can be rationalized to mean progress. But what ought to be done? What ought we to expect of ourselves and others? How shall we measure the quality of our relationships and our individual part in them?

Until the 1960s, schools, entertainment media, religion, laws and the courts, and society in general swept everyone along toward a generally accepted goal—the traditional family. Even the financial structure encouraged home buying and one-wage-earner families, thus encouraging mothers to "rock the cradle" and thereby nurture each upcoming generation. Under this pervasive influence most people just went along with the flow: they courted, married, had children, became grandparents, and expected their children to respect, if not repeat, the same cycle. Divorce was frowned on. For a man and woman to live together without marrying was wicked. The process of creating and maintaining relationships was taken for granted.

Today, however, we can take very little for granted. Many people grow up without clear examples of enduring relationships. Far too many are unwilling to work and work hard to build and preserve marriages and families. They too easily, too casually "resign" because the task is difficult. Anyone who wants to enrich or heal a troubled relationship must analyze, evaluate, plan, and work at it, and work and work. But the rewards are profound when we work intelligently and earnestly on relationships.

The various people I have known who have been successful in this have done so in steps or phases that can be labeled, in order of priority, _self-definition_, _self-discipline_, and _self-understanding._ They decided who they were and who they wanted to be—they *defined* themselves. Then they worked to control their thoughts, impulses, attitudes, and actions—they *disciplined* themselves. Finally, they took the time and made the effort to search their hearts and personal histories enough to get to know the inner person behind the outer facade—they *understood* themselves. The result of these three steps was that they learned with accuracy what to expect of themselves in a relationship and how to give of themselves in it. And because they gave, in most cases they received. Not in all cases, of course, for real human relationships are not like fairy tales or television scripts. They are at once tougher, sweeter, sadder, and more joyous than any fiction could possibly portray. And, yes, usually the giver becomes also a receiver.

As you read this book, you may be in one of the following situations: You are an adult. Your parents are still difficult to understand. You want to improve your relationship with them because you recognize that with each passing year, instead of lessening, the need to understand and relate to your parents increases.

You are or were a victim of abuse. Several years after the event or events, you have a conflict between anger at the perpetrator and longing for a reconciliation.

You are dating and considering marriage but are very concerned about the risks of marriage.

You are newly married. Things are going well and you want to keep it that way.

You have been married for years, and your relationship with your spouse seems to be in a deteriorating pattern.

Or, good as it may seem by comparison with others, you feel that your marriage relationship could and should be improved.

Experience suggests that most people could profit by applying the three-step process this book sets forth. Those who are serious about defining, disciplining, and understanding themselves so as to prepare for or enhance or heal relationships must be willing to gather the necessary information and then assess the correctness of their beliefs, their values, and their behavior. Armed with the information, a person can form expectations of himself or herself and of others, as well as accept others' expectations of him or her, with a high degree of confidence about whether such expectations are correct and beneficial. In short, a person can decide accurately, confidently, what he or she ought to contribute to and expect from a relationship, whatever the other person does. This does not guarantee that the relationship will succeed, but it does ensure that at least one of the two persons will do everything possible to give it a chance to succeed.

As we set out, it will be necessary to keep in mind a severe reality about our time and its relationships. The values and practices that influence far too many relationships today are as transitory as the season's most popular television show or movie. Many modern forces undermine relationships. Certain laws and customs actually denigrate, even oppose, formal, enduring relationships. Under such an onslaught many falter. Some come from troubled homes or from families in which the members merely coexisted, with no particular warmth or richness of spirit and relationship. And some are even victims of abuse. What this adds up to is that most of us need to learn how to enrich relationships that, while basically sound, nevertheless are unusually stressed by the lack of societal support for enduring relationships. Others of us need to heal wounds lest our already troubled relationships sicken further and die.

Basic to this book are certain verities which, after many years of personal and professional efforts to understand what blesses and what damages human relationships, I accept as law. Among them are these: Kindliness in one's childhood home begets kindliness in the home a person establishes as an adult. When a father is a diligent breadwinner, probably so will his sons be and his daughters will expect it of their husbands. When the mother learns and practices the domestic arts, her children will appreciate them in their selection of spouses. Family prayer and scripture study add strength to family relationships. Special qualities are usually formed in the marriage relationships of a man and woman who court each other according to the laws of chastity and virtue.

The benefits of this life-style are incalculable. Prophets have taught us these truths through the ages.

That the enriching or healing efforts discussed in this book are necessary even for people who know and strive to live the gospel of Jesus Christ should not surprise people who seek a personal relationship with the Redeemer of all mankind. He is the personification of love. He does not wait for us to love him; rather "We love him, because he first loved us" (1 John 4:19).

The living of gospel principles prepares us for good human relationships. But none of us is perfect; most of us falter, and some suffer from harmful relationships. It is because of these realities that this book attempts to offer an organized way to enrich or heal significant relationships through self-definition, self-discipline, and self-understanding. For you and I have the responsibility, even the power, to accomplish this enriching or healing to a degree limited only by the other person's agency but always enhanced by the grace of Christ.

*That we henceforth be no
more children, tossed to and
fro, and carried about with
every wind of doctrine, . . .
but speaking the truth in love,
may grow up into him in all
things, which is the head,
even Christ.*
— *Ephesians 4:14–15*

Where Is Truth?

CHAPTER TWO

Edward had dated several women before courting and then marrying Arvella. They enjoyed a modest two-day honeymoon on limited funds. Through their early years together they struggled to put Edward through college even as three children were born. As the years rolled by, their family grew until there were seven children. Despite the inevitable alternations of trials and successes, each passing year marked a deepening of the couple's relationship.

Simply put, Edward and Arvella had learned and practiced certain bedrock principles and laws of human relationships. Similarly, each of us has it within his power to enrich relationships by knowing and applying correct principles. Conversely, if we fail to heed these principles we will almost invariably harm relationships. Even in the latter case we can heal the relationship if we will apply the very principles we have neglected. Either situation requires that we take the time and commit ourselves to the task.

At age thirty-two, Priscilla was considering divorcing her husband, but she had serious anxieties. How would she provide for her three children? Was there a man out there for her who would be a better husband and father than her present husband? Was she up to marrying again? Were there ways to save the present marriage? If there were, how long would it take? And could she endure it for that long? Where could she get some reliable information to work with? In fact, what are the sources of truth by which Edward, Arvella, Priscilla, and the rest of us can guide our relationships?

Among the sources of correct principles and practices are family and general history, the human sciences, observations of others, time-tested (not merely traditional) values, and religious covenants. In seeking sources of truth we ought to be motivated both by the wisdom in scripture and the knowledge in good secular books. We may reasonably apply to ourselves the instruction to "study and learn, and become acquainted with all good books, and with languages, tongues, and peoples" (D&C 90:14–15), and nowhere is this more important than in the field of human relationships.

Before we move ahead to the specifics of self-definition, self-discipline, and self-understanding, then, let us take time to consider the usefulness of reliable sources of knowledge that lead to truth.

Family and General History

Failure to know which ideas and practices about human behavior have passed the rigorous tests of time can condemn us to repeat errors in relationships. Many kinds of historical sources give us valuable help. They include diaries, personal journals, letters, biographies, and formal histories. Obviously we cannot call time-out to study the history of mankind while we are in the throes of a personal relationship decision, but unless we choose to flail about reactively we must at the very least make the effort to measure our beliefs and behaviors against the historical perspectives of other people.

Among the richest potential sources of insight are letters, poems, and diaries. When a person writes of his or her private emotions and experiences such writing often provides kernels of raw truth, perceptions and insights that are diluted neither by the work of editors nor by the formal training of historians. This book draws on such records.

Throughout this book too we will refer to biographical sources. Some are private. Several are from the lives of public figures, about whom much tends to be revealed. They perform in front of people. They are interviewed many times over. They write autobiographies or others write biographies of them. If their careers last very long we see them change over time. The lives and relationships of such as monarchs, politicians, entertainers, and religious leaders usually are well documented and often are interesting as well as informative.

Thucydides, a Greek historian of the fifth century B.C., succinctly justified using history as a guide for human affairs. "If [my history] be judged useful by those inquirers who desire an exact knowledge of the past as an aid to the interpretation of the future . . . I shall be content" (*The History of the Peloponnesian War*, in *Great Books of the Western World* [Chicago: Encyclopaedia Britannica, 1952], vol. 6, p. 354). This measurement of usefulness applies equally to homey diaries and scholarly tomes.

Will and Ariel Durant cautioned us to have a prudent respect for history: "No man, however brilliant or well-informed, can come in one lifetime to such fullness of understanding as to safely judge and dismiss the customs or institutions of his society, for these are the wisdom of generations after centuries of experiment in the laboratory of history" (*The Lessons of History* [New York: Simon and Schuster, 1968], pp. 35–36). For example, history teaches that for a society to treat marital and family relationships lightly is to sow seeds of destruction. Invaluable if imperfect sources about this aspect of the ancient past include formal histories such as Edward Gibbon's *Decline and Fall of the Roman Empire*, but we need not always look to long-dead societies for historical perspective about human relationships. Terribly urgent examples exist today.

One such example is seen in the attempt, commendable in its intent, to alleviate the economic distress of needy women and children. In the United States a vast welfare system has evolved

IT FOSTERS WHAT IT "CORRECTS".!

from this effort. Unfortunately a large part of it restricts help to households from which the husband is absent. Increasingly there appears to be a correlation between this particular kind of financial assistance and the deterioration of certain family relationships. It has taken only fifty years of historical evaluation to verify this trend.

History enjoins moderation even upon zealots. Neither liberalism nor conservativism, organized religion nor organized irreligion, can afford to ignore the historical imperatives about human relationships. Such imperatives do not yield to modern man's often self-serving illusions as to right and wrong—they resist "them that call evil good and good evil" (Isaiah 5:20).

Allan Bloom speaks to this theme in his provocative book *The Closing of the American Mind.* "It is important to emphasize that the lesson the students [of today] are drawing from their studies is simply untrue. History and the study of cultures do not teach or prove that values or cultures are relative. All to the contrary. . . . The fact that there have been different opinions about good and bad in different times and places in no way proves that none is true or superior to others. . . . History and anthropology cannot provide the answers, but they can provide the material on which judgment can work." (*The Closing of the American Mind* [New York: Simon and Schuster, 1987], pp. 39-40.)

From modern revelation too we may conclude that it is well to pay heed to the lessons of history: "And, verily I say unto you, that it is my will that you should . . . obtain a knowledge of history, and of countries, and of kingdoms, of laws of God and man, and all this for the salvation of Zion" (D&C 93:53; see also 88:78–79).

Clearly, the use of various historical sources can provide material by which each of us can and needs to judge right and wrong, usefulness or uselessness, blessing or harm in our relationships.

Human Sciences

By letting the facts speak for themselves the human sciences have exposed many myths about relationships and have verified certain truths. For example, in the early twentieth century considerable debate was engendered about how to toilet-train children;

in an era before disposable diapers this aspect of parent-child relations was no minor issue. A fairly widespread type of moderate
child abuse by frustrated parents occurred around harsh "potty
training," and in response or reaction there arose from child
psychology a more casual approach. Yet this permissive approach
failed to accomplish the necessary results any better than the
stricter way. Eventually research determined that it was the relationship factor that counted most: If the parent conveyed approval and acceptance, then the child tried to achieve control of
sphincter and bladder. If the parent rejected the child, the child
failed or learned slowly in the end and was conflicted.

Unfortunately the actions of some social science commentators
also have proved detrimental to human relationships, in that they
apostatized from true methodology by refusing to allow for the
personal bias that can influence collection and interpretation of
data. (See L. E. Bentler, M. Crago, T. G. Arizmendi, "Therapist
Variables in Psychotherapy Process and Outcome," in *Handbook
of Psychotherapy and Behavior Change*, ed. Sol L. Garfield, Allen
E. Bergin [New York: John Wiley and Sons, 1986], pp. 257–310 —
particularly pp. 273–76.) The comments of syndicated columnist
Joan Beck, in her review of a book that extolled the enjoyment of
sex without marriage or creating a family, points us to an example
of such bias.

> What women have won, the authors say, is a redefinition of
> sex that is "more compatible" with their "broader erotic possibili-
> ties." They have also managed to decouple sex from grander ideas
> of eternal love, romance and "surrender" that "were there in part
> to distract us from the paucity of pleasure." They want sex to
> have no ultimate meaning other than pleasure and no "great mys-
> tery except how to achieve it." And they cheer that women have
> achieved this goal. . . .
>
> Arguments like these must have brought the authors — and
> much of the feminist movement — to a realistic and ideological
> dead end. They have also cost the support of millions of women
> who enthusiastically share the goals of enjoying a full range of
> sexual pleasure and intimacy but find that impossible if sex is di-
> vorced from meaning and commitment.
>
> There is nothing inherent in a good marriage or in having
> children that precludes a full and joyous experience of sexuality,

however unlikely that may seem to the authors of this book. (*Sacramento Union*, 5 October 1986, p. A19.)

One of the most dramatic results of professional bias that has influenced public policy is seen in increased teenage pregnancies and sexually transmitted diseases. The bias consisted in the conviction that increased sexual information *without values* would reduce detrimental consequences. Indeed, numbers of live births have decreased, but abortions have increased as have irresponsible sexual activity and out-of-wedlock pregnancies. (See Stan E. Weed, "Effects of Family Planning Programs on Teenage Pregnancy," Paper for the U. S. Senate Committee on Labor and Human Resources, 30 July 1987.)

Another frequent defect or bias in the conclusions of social scientists is their ignoring of spiritual considerations. Reason, logic, intellect — these are honorable tools of mankind, but they do not explain the spirit. In our day, when many "old-fashioned virtues" have been discarded, we have very few constraints on behavior. Except for blatant violence, almost anything is tolerated. Many are living in the way that ancient Greek philosophers proposed mankind ought to, that is, according to each individual's unique, unfettered reason. They create their own gods and their own rituals of worship. The gods of the human sciences are worshipped by words, writings, and debates. Under this philosophy, of primary import is the intellectual process and the rigor of the effort.

If this approach included all knowledge it could have a high degree of reliability, but to our grave danger this is not the case. Most of the studies conducted exclude religion and values. This exclusion may be of lesser consequence in the case of the physical sciences, but in that of the social sciences it amounts to a disregard for vast areas of human relationships.

Despite this drawback, however, when used judiciously the human sciences and their methods can be helpful. For example, clinical reports describe the formal efforts of the human sciences to heal relationships, and thus they tend to balance the subjectivity and perhaps inaccessibility of biographies. Clifford and Marie's misunderstanding, summarized in chapter 1, is a case in point. Had that been just noted in a personal journal entry we might not have the clinical benefit of their lessons about retaining bad memories too long and about avoiding undue dependence on others.

Observation

One day an intelligent, middle-aged, single man finally asked me a question he should have asked long before: "How can I learn some ways to relate better with other people?" In response I urged him to observe what other people do and from that to adopt or adapt what seemed useful. Watching others is an endless, easy, and quite reliable source of information. It can be done in the supermarket, at church, at work or school, in any public place, or even in the home — though in the home, making objective observations is often difficult.

A teenage daughter's apparent disregard of parental advice drove her parents to seek counsel. The solution was partly clinical and partly a matter of observation. I asked them if the daughter ever paid heed to their counsel. They weren't sure of the answer, so they observed her over a two-week period and discovered that when they offered their opinion *once* and then said no more about the matter their daughter *usually* accepted counsel. (*Always* is not a safe term to use in describing human behavior.) When they persisted — that is, nagged — she *usually* rejected their views. This observation proved to be valuable — the parents adjusted their behavior accordingly, and as a consequence their daughter became more cooperative.

What others do, and when, how, and why they do it, are data we should all continually gather as we learn to improve our own relationship behavior.

Time-Tested Values

We have already noted briefly the importance of values in our relationships. Values are not just interesting, they are also practical. Values are beliefs we act upon. To speak of our values and yet fail to act on them relegates them to the status of mere wishes or, in some unhappy instances, indicates hypocrisy.

Not all values have a positive effect. Some are morally offensive in their consequences. Mafia relationships, for example, are based on values of secrecy that promote and protect prostitution, extortion, pornography, and murder. And Mafiosi *do* act on their values.

These days, illusion permeates society. On every hand we are enticed to adopt the values of "openness" or "tolerance," and anything firmer is likely to be labeled prejudice or intolerance. But what should properly motivate and govern our relationships? The last thing that people with troubled relationships need is valueless pap. They are starved, and only nourishment will save their emotional lives. Neither do they need dead traditions, such as the traditional male tyranny that has created the enormous discontent that boils among women today. They need proper values, values that provide nourishment for the spirit. Purposeful, value-based achievements in relationships, especially those of our Judeo-Christian heritage, warm hearts and increase self-confidence. (For reliable human science references on values and religion the reader may want to review especially the various articles by Allen E. Bergin, e.g., "Religious Life-Styles and Mental Health: An Exploratory Study," *Journal of Counseling Psychology*, 1988, vol. 35, no. 1, pp. 91–98.)

Malcolm Muggeridge, prominent English writer, editor, and radio and television personality, embraced Christianity late in life and caught the significance of its values. He wrote: "In light of contemporary attitudes, it must seem extraordinary that so much joy could have come of Jesus's seemingly harsh exigencies, whereas the return to pagan permissiveness has spread a dreadful gloom and boredom over the Western world." (*Jesus, the Man Who Lives*, p. 123. Copyright © 1975 by Malcolm Muggeridge. Reprinted by permission of Harper and Row.)

For nearly six thousand years the basis for Judeo-Christian values has been that a Father in Heaven sent us here to decide for ourselves how we want to live hereafter. Believers anticipate reporting to him and his Son at some future time. As William Barclay of Glasgow University put it, believers in "the Christian ethic ought never to forget that men have bodies and these bodies are the property of God and that they matter to God. . . . The Christian ethic lives in the consciousness of eternity." (*Ethics in a Permissive Society* [London: Harper and Row, 1971], p. 39.)

While acknowledging our human weaknesses, our failure to practice fully the Christian values we have espoused, what would our society be like—our workplaces, our families, our intimate relationships—without the Christlike values of kindness, patience, service, sacrifice, justice, honesty, respect for the body, and veneration of truth and beauty?

Where in all literature are finer values than those Jesus taught in the Beatitudes—that our relationships ought to be characterized by humility, meekness, mercy, purity of heart, peace, integrity?

But there is more to true religion than values. There are covenants.

Religious Covenants

While traveling in Japan several years ago I was struck by the decline of traditional religion there—Shinto and Buddhism. This decline opened a tremendous gap in the values of the people and in their relationships. Materialism and Western variations of Christianity competed to fill the vacuum.

A similar observation could no doubt be made of other countries. If this were a book which merely presented a potpourri of views, it would review various cultures, their histories and their religions, and draw no conclusions. But its intent instead is to consider those ideas, attitudes, and actions that have enriched or healed specific relationships involving people who, being Latter-day Saints, believed in the priesthood covenants God has given to his people through living prophets.

Because of the terrible abuses that have been both suffered and inflicted by adherents of organized religion, social scientists and many others have been rightly wary of formal religions. In our effort here to point to ways that enhance and heal relationships, we shall therefore embrace a specific and personal religious fact that transcends sectarian dogma and tradition. This is the intimate, covenant relationship between Jesus Christ and those who believe in him. In this book, that will be our definition of ultimate religion.

The term *covenant*, as it applies to our discussion, was defined by Moses: "And [Moses] took the book of the covenant, and read in the audience of the people: and they said, All that the Lord hath said will we do, and be obedient" (Exodus 24:7).

As we speak of covenants that affect human relationships we mean solemn obligations defined by God. Our fidelity to these obligations brings upon us God's approval and blessings. This must not be confused with the inconsistent, often conditional approval that mortal fathers are prone to give, even as a means by which to manipulate their children. It is the unconditional love of an all-knowing, all-loving Father in Heaven who "so loved the world that he gave his only begotten Son, that whosoever believeth in him should not perish, but have everlasting life" (John 3:16). Late in life, after he gave himself to Christianity, Malcolm Muggeridge described the importance of and the historical disregard for Jesus:

> Apart from the one dubious reference in Josephus, in his own lifetime Jesus made no impact on [formal] history. This is something that I cannot but regard as a special dispensation on God's part, and, I like to think, yet another example of the ironical humor which informs so many of His purposes. To me, it seems highly appropriate that the most important figure in all history should thus escape the notice of memoirists, diarists, commentators, all the tribe of chroniclers who even then existed. . . . Historically, Jesus is, strictly speaking, a non-person. Anthropologically, too, he is without interest; we know, in this respect, more about Neanderthal Man than about the Son of Man.

Having said this, Muggeridge explains the significance to him of a personal relationship with Jesus: "The only way to be sane about history is to keep its end in view, as the only way to be sane about living is to keep death in view. Jesus catered for this need by promising to return to us, and soon rather than late, so that we should be under the necessity of always expecting him." And again, "I hear those words: '*I am the resurrection, and the life,*' and feel myself to be carried along on a great tide of joy and peace." (*Jesus, the Man Who Lives,* pp. 23, 95, 100. See copyright and permission information, page 15 herein.)

Why would anyone who professes belief in or even mere awareness of Jesus Christ exclude him from their studies of human relationships? In searching for truth about relationships it makes little sense for a serious seeker to set aside ideas, experiences, values, laws, and covenants that are claimed to originate with God the Father and his only begotten Son. To be sure, there is a challenge in trying to determine what men have mistranslated or corrupted and what is the pure word of God. But can this sorting out remotely justify even nonreligious people in ignoring the teachings, history, and impact of the Teacher whose life and teachings have touched or shaped the lives of billions in a positive way?

It is only too obvious that historically the Christian ideal and the Christian practice have most often been far apart. As Edward Gibbon stated: "The theologian may indulge the pleasing task of describing Religion as she descended from Heaven, arrayed in her native purity. A more melancholy duty is imposed on the historian. He must discover the inevitable mixture of error and corruption which she contracted in a long residence upon earth, among a weak and degenerate race of beings." (*The Decline and Fall of the Roman Empire*, vol. 1 [New York: Modern Library, n.d.], pp. 382–83.)

This discrepancy between principle and practice is the reason why throughout this book I use the term *religion* to mean the doctrines and covenants given to mankind by Jesus Christ, as recorded in scripture by prophets and Apostles.

Most of the people whose experiences appear in this book base their values about relationships on the life, gospel, and covenants of Jesus Christ, the God of Abraham, Isaac, and Jacob, the Messiah, the Redeemer. But even sacred covenants do not eliminate human weakness or isolate people from trials and difficulties. The beliefs and struggles of those in this book are relevant to Paul's anguished yet comforting words:

> For that which I do I allow not: for what I would, that do I not; but what I hate, that do I. If then I do that which I would not, I consent unto the law that it is good . . . for I delight in the law of God after the inward man: but I see another law in my members, warring against the law of my mind, and bringing me into captivity to the law of sin which is in my members. O wretched man that I am! who shall deliver me from the body of this death? I thank God through Jesus Christ our Lord. So then with the mind I myself serve the law of God; but with the flesh the law of sin. (Romans 7:15–16, 22–25.)

Paul's lament is also a declaration of religious intent. Even though his "members" or body parts sometimes war against his spirit, he vows to persist in the struggle to become righteous, to overcome the world as did his Exemplar.

The religion of the Son of God, then, as we shall refer to it, consists of covenants between the Father and his sons and daughters, with the Son as Mediator and Redeemer. The Atonement is God's ultimate token of keeping his covenant with us. The Old Testament prophesied of it. The New Testament witnessed it.

Covenants with God are either to be acted upon or rejected. Once entered into, they cannot be ignored. Perhaps this is why Jesus said, "So then because thou art lukewarm, and neither cold nor hot, I will spue thee out of my mouth" (Revelation 3:16).

Knowledge and conviction, then, are central to this covenant relationship. God cannot reveal his laws to prophets and send his only begotten Son to redeem mankind yet at the same time be a figment of the imagination or an image interpretable by varying opinions. Either God the Father is or he is not. Either Jesus is or he is not. In this connection C. S. Lewis wrote:

> I am trying here to prevent anyone saying the really foolish thing that people often say about Him: "I'm ready to accept Jesus as a great moral teacher, but I don't accept His claim to be God." That is the one thing we must not say. A man who was merely a man and said the sort of things Jesus said would not be a great moral teacher. He would either be a lunatic — on a level with the man who says he is a poached egg — or else he would be the Devil of Hell. You must make your choice. Either this man was, and is, the Son of God; or else a madman or something worse. You can shut Him up for a fool, you can spit at Him and kill Him as a demon; or you can fall at His feet and call Him Lord and God. But let us not come with any patronising nonsense about His being a great human teacher. He has not left that open to us. He did not intend to. (C. S. Lewis, *Mere Christianity* [London: Collins Fount, 1960], pp. 55–56.)

If we are to examine God's word to the Hebrews and the early Christians, what is our basic document? It is the Holy Bible, and for our English-speaking purposes that means the King James or the Authorized Version. Muggeridge says it well: "The new translations of the Bible, each, as it seems to me [is], stylistically speaking, more flat and unprofitable than the last. . . . We whose language is English may rejoice that in our Authorized Version we have a translation of incomparable artistry and luminosity." (*Jesus, the Man Who Lives*, pp. 8–9. See copyright and permission information, page 15 herein.)

If believers are to drink of Judeo-Christian doctrines that pertain to relationships, they must draw them from as pure a well as possible. Most wells that have been dug since the Apostles of the first century are polluted in varying degrees. Because it has been compiled, copied, and translated by fallible men, the Bible, as invaluable as it is, cannot conceivably be complete. Thus we need to gather information from the scriptures and all other possible sources, evaluate it, pray for guidance, and then listen to the Holy Spirit as we make decisions about relationships.

In particular, the follower of Christ needs to be a seeker of current revelation. In this connection there is a poignant and interesting story about the Christian philosopher-theologian Thomas Aquinas (approximately A.D. 1225-1274). He wrote prolifically, densely, and earnestly quite like Aristotle. His life was dedicated to exposition of Christian theology. On 6 December 1273 he abruptly ceased to write. By his own account, while saying mass a great change came over him. "Such things have been revealed to me," he said, "that all I have written seems as straw, and I now await the end of my life" (*Great Books of the Western World*, vol. 19 [Chicago: Encyclopaedia Britannica, 1952], p. vi). In this experience Thomas Aquinas apparently discovered for himself a truth that Gibbon would infer hundreds of years later: "Since therefore the most sublime efforts of philosophy can extend no farther than feebly to point out the desire, the hope, or, at most, the probability of a future state, there is nothing except a divine revelation that can ascertain the existence and describe the condition of the invisible country which is destined to receive the souls of men after their separation from the body" (*Decline and Fall*, vol. 1, p. 399).

In our day divine revelation comes both from written scripture and from living prophets. The Book of Mormon, the Doctrine and Covenants, and the Pearl of Great Price are just what good people such as Thomas Aquinas yearn for. They give us truth about covenant human relationships as they bridge the whole span of human history. In addition we are blessed with the timely pronouncements of living prophets.

Jesus Christ is the source of the religion that influenced most of those whose experiences are reported in this book. In turn, he did what his Father taught him: "I do nothing of myself; but as my Father hath taught me, I speak these things. . . . for I do always

Jesus answered them,
Is it not written in your
law, I said, Ye are gods?
— John 10:34

Self-Definition

CHAPTER THREE

Christmas can be the most nostalgic of all seasons. During that season we expect the best from others and from ourselves. Also we see the vast contrast between what can be and what actually is, what is noble and sacred and what is ignoble and profane.

One Christmas Eve, around midnight, a woman phoned me long-distance. She did not give her name. She had just read my book *Human Intimacy* and wanted some advice about her relationship with her current boyfriend. What struck me as she told her story was her utter lack of confidence. She spoke offhandedly of various achievements in life —college, career, interesting avocations —but she spoke emphatically about how fearful she was of losing her friend. I inferred from all she related in our hour's conversation that she was a capable, effective person in most areas except in matters of the heart.

One week later, on New Year's Eve, I received another long-distance phone call. This time it was a man calling, a man in deep despair. Criticism he had received that day from his wife had depressed him badly and had also upset his two children.

Seasons of nostalgia had moved these two lonely people to brood that they would never be loved.

These two instances demonstrate how important it is for people to take responsibility for their relationships by defining themselves, especially before they enter into intimate relationships. The associations we yearn for will not develop until we come to terms with ourselves. Time and again people seek in vain to be loved, failing to understand that even though others can contribute to our problems, we often plant our own seeds of failure by expecting or hoping that someone else will create a relationship for us. Such expectations can lead to pessimism, inconsistency, anxiety, dependence, obsession, and desperation.

The profound need we all have for human relationships is more likely to be met by our own efforts than by waiting for others to create them. Hence the practicality of self-definition.

Pogo said it well: "We have met the enemy and he is us."

Self-definition begins as we accept responsibility for our own attitudes and behaviors. It flourishes as we decide who and what we will be and as we set out to act accordingly. Along the way we improve our ability to relate to other people, respect their needs, and appreciate them for what they are, not for what we require them to be.

Suggestions about how to go about defining oneself will be given in the following chapters, but first it is necessary to lay out for your consideration why self-definition is worth the effort.

Cary Grant offers intriguing evidence. Yes, the actor who died in 1986. Two magazine articles — one written before and one after his death — paint a picture.

The first article is the somewhat cynical account by a writer assigned to review the actor's one-man stage show that he gave around the United States until shortly before he died. The advertisements invited customers "to know more about the man behind the ideal." The writer professes himself unclear why his editor and three thousand other people would each pay fifteen dollars that evening for "A Conversation with Cary Grant."

> Throughout the evening Mr. Grant remains genial and completely at ease, almost as if he's enjoying himself. He seems

slightly bemused by all the attention he's being paid, particularly since he himself has nothing in particular he wishes to impart, and except for his amazing state of preservation, appears to be otherwise unremarkable. In short, he is polished, graceful, urbane, beautifully dressed and very handsome. In short, he is Cary Grant. . . .

Leave us with our illusions. We worship screen idols for the same reason we worship gods — they are eternal, they won't go away and leave us. And Cary Grant, vigorous, virile, more handsome than ever at 81, is confirmation that our devotions are not in vain. If the real Cary Grant was ever anybody other than that icon we remembered from *Notorious, To Catch a Thief, North by Northwest, Charade*, then we don't want to know about it. The emotional revelation implied by a face behind the mask was never a feature of his performing art anyway; he was just the simple perfection of manner and style. (Page Stegner, "The Archaeology of Cary Grant," *California Magazine*, December 1986, pp. 97, 105.)

But the question is, Was it a mask *by the time of his death?* Here is what one obituary reported:

Better than anyone else, Grant understood that his public persona was a fiction, and a highly stylized one at that. "Everyone wants to be Cary Grant," he liked to say. "*I* want to be Cary Grant." Indeed, in a strange way, it had been his lifelong ambition, though at first he could not have given a name to his goal or, as he also admitted, define it with any accuracy. "I don't know that I've any style at all," he once told an interviewer. "I just patterned myself on a combination of Jack Buchanan [a debonair English musical-comedy star of the '20s and '30s], Noel Coward and Rex Harrison. I pretended to be somebody I wanted to be, and I finally became that person. Or he became me. Or we met at some point." . . .

What he seemed to be saying was that he had not yet purified those performances of autobiography, had not yet completed the process of total reinvention that was the largest promise acting held out to him as a young man. Born Archibald Leach in bleak Bristol, England, son of a drinking, defeated father and a mother who was placed in a madhouse when he was ten, he was a lonely, latchkey child, who decided on a life in show biz the first time he visited backstage. "A dazzling land of smiling, jostling people . . . classless, cheerful and carefree," is how he later described what he saw.

His first job, at age 14, confirmed his hunch, for he caught on with Bob Pender, who managed a troupe of boy acrobats as if it were a kindly, disciplined, extended family. Young Archie learned acrobatics, mime and, above all, the joys of camaraderie and the need for collegial generosity. At the height of his career, he would remain the least narcissistic of actors, always willing to share scenes and to take a chance with some undignified business if someone thought it would work. . . .

This last is what people came to know best in recent years. It was the logical extension of his screen character as he had finally refined it, a healthy spirit who kept his troubles and even his memories to himself. (Richard Schickel, *"The Acrobat of the Drawing Room," Time*, 15 December 1986, p. 95. Copyright 1986 Time Inc. Reprinted by permission.)

It seems clear, then, that in a thoroughly documented way Cary Grant transformed himself by self-definition.* Or, more precisely, he built successfully on certain elements of his inborn personality, acquired various character traits, and literally acted himself into the person he wanted to become. "I pretended to be somebody I wanted to be, and I finally became that person." (This process is described in chapter 5.)

The *self* in self-definition cannot be too strongly emphasized. A person who truly defines himself or herself does not rely unduly upon others for affirmation. The steps he takes, which are described in later chapters, are primarily self-directed steps. No one else can take them for us. Obviously, others have a constant and considerable influence on our lives, but whether *they* decide what or who we ought to be is the crucial point. There is no question but that each individual needs to make that decision for himself.

To accomplish this a person must at times exercise a stern determination not to enter into what could become a problem relationship, or to emancipate himself from a detrimental, long-standing relationship. George Bernard Shaw's play *Pygmalion* portrayed such a change. The grand secret of *Pygmalion* was not that egocentric Henry Higgins transformed Eliza Doolittle, the

---

*My father served on a corporate board with Cary Grant and found him to be as charming off screen as he was on screen.

Cockney flower girl, but that she did it herself. True, in the beginning she utilized his technical skills to improve her speech and social abilities. But with increasing power she took control of the relationship.

> HIGGINS. You know, Pickering, that woman has the most extraordinary ideas about me. Here I am, a shy, diffident sort of man. I've never been able to feel really grown-up and tremendous, like other chaps. And yet she's firmly persuaded that I'm an arbitrary overbearing bossing kind of person. I can't account for it!

Much later, after Eliza has been hurt by Higgins's inhumane use of her in society to win a bet, she begins the process of emancipation. The trigger is Professor Higgins's search for his slippers.

> HIGGINS. What did you throw those slippers at me for?

> LIZA. Because I wanted to smash your face. I'd like to kill you, you selfish brute. Why didn't you leave me where you picked me out of — in the gutter?

Liza leaves in anger and pain but returns several days later and, under the protection of Professor Higgins's mother, resumes the dialogue, this time speaking to Colonel Pickering in Higgins's hearing.

> LIZA (to Pickering). Do you know what began my real education? . . . You calling me Miss Doolittle . . . that was the beginning of self-respect for me. And there were a hundred little things you never noticed, because they came naturally to you. Things like standing up and taking off your hat and opening doors — .

Then she begins to redefine her self and her relationships.

> PICKERING. Well, this is really very nice of you, Miss Doolittle.

> LIZA. I should like you to call me Eliza, now, if you would. And I should like Professor Higgins to call me Miss Doolittle.

> HIGGINS. I'll see you damned first.

The professor launches a vituperous attack but Eliza stands her ground.

Finally Eliza assumes responsibility for the relationship as she casts off Higgins's domination and begins to define herself.

> LIZA. Oh, when I think of myself crawling under your feet and being trampled on and called names, when all the time I had only to lift up my finger [her little finger daintily lifted while sipping from her tea cup] to be as good as you. I could kick myself.

Whereupon Eliza Doolittle, in the playwright's words, "becomes cool and elegant" and departs calmly, even regally, for church with the professor's mother. (George Bernard Shaw, *Androcles and the Lion, Overruled, Pygmalion* [New York: Dodd, Mead and Company, 1930], pp. 107–224.)

A similar transformation began abruptly before my eyes early in my clinical work. A profoundly disturbed woman had come to several counseling sessions, but I did not possess the skill to help her. Only her intense lack of self-esteem blinded her to my professional inadequacy. In her youth she had been quite attractive and desperate for acceptance and had used her allure as the basis of relationships with boys and men. Eventually she became a bedraggled plaything for wicked men, which her demeanor and grooming showed.

Her problems were greater than was my experience, and I knew it. I had decided to transfer her to someone else and intended to tell her this at the next session.

Ordinarily I went out into the waiting room to escort clients in, but this time she walked into my office while I sat at my desk doing last-minute paper work. As she entered, I automatically stood up to greet her. The expression on her face baffled me. She slowly sank into the chair and began to weep quietly. After a time I asked what was wrong. She softly answered: "It has been a long, long time since a man showed me respect. When you stood up I realized you respected me." And from that point on she began to heal. Even through several crises she behaved as if she now knew something finer about herself.

A person who defines herself as worthy of respect is usually able to enhance her relationships. She expects courtesy, kindness, and fidelity. To such a person the first ugly word is offensive; physical abuse is an intolerable violation that ends the budding relationship; selfishness is recognized as a slow-acting poison. She recognizes that it is dangerous to marry a troubled person with the expectation of reforming him—if there is a diamond hidden inside, the rocky exterior can be removed before marriage; that is a prudent and decent course. To deliberately take the risk of marrying and then trying to reform the partner is folly, and has broken many tender, well-intentioned hearts. Inevitably, however, there are relationships in which the partner's problems were not obvious until later, and these need to be healed.

The display of common decency has the power to warm the hearts and lift the despair of those among us who have lost most if not all of their self-esteem. It is true that in this less-than-best of all possible worlds we cannot count on being treated decently, especially when we are perceived as vulnerable. But as we consider *self*-definition we should not ignore the power of kind treatment by and to others. The entire world looks better if someone cares for us. And more readily we can believe in and hope for a better relationship if we do for others what we ourselves yearn to have done for us. Isaiah and Paul both taught this, and the Savior reaffirmed it in our day: "Lift up the hands which hang down, and strengthen the feeble knees" (D&C 81:5; see also Isaiah 35:3; Hebrews 12:12).

It is a redeeming act when someone lifts us up as we droop. (Even when someone else cares intensely, however, life does not allow such support forever; nor is permanent support healthy, for the resulting dependence would cripple us.) Self-definition is aided by kindness from others; that almost always revives a careworn heart. Notice, however, that the person treated with kindness must recognize it and be willing to accept it. My rising as the client came in was not an intentionally therapeutic act; it was habit. She chose to see it in a way that opened a door to healing.

Consider one last example from popular literature and the stage. It is Aldonza's song from *Man of La Mancha*, the musical presentation of *Don Quixote*. This is the same play that features "The Impossible Dream," but Aldonza's song may be the truer tale. It reveals the turmoil of a human heart that is beginning to thaw in the hope that there is worth within, the heart of someone who has long accepted her place as an object of sexual contempt. By her self-hatred Aldonza had controlled the men who paid for her sexual favors.

Don Quixote de la Mancha, in his addled but noble defense of goodness and truth, sees Aldonza not as a fallen woman but as *Dulcinea*, a gentlewoman of virtue. He calls her by this new name and treats her accordingly. She begins to believe. This makes her vulnerable, though, because she no longer hates herself. Now her former customers viciously ridicule her. Don Quixote comes upon her shortly after she has been humiliated and addresses her as "My lady." She turns on him with all the venom and despair of one who had dared to hope, only to be crushed. First she cries in rejection of her admirer's absurd belief: "I am not your lady. I am not any kind of a lady!" This she follows by a bitter recounting of her illegitimate birth and her subsequent sordid life. Don Quixote, disbelieving, persists in addressing her as "My lady."

Aldonza moans: "And still he torments me! How should I be a lady?" She continues her ugly biography. Her final outburst reveals utter self-contempt:

"Take the clouds from your eyes and see me as I really am. You have shown me the sky, but what good is the sky to a creature who'll never do better than crawl.

"Of all the cruel [devils] who've badgered and battered me, you are the cruelest of all.

"Can't you see what your gentle insanities do to me; rob me of anger and give me despair?

"Blows and abuse I can take and give back again. Tenderness I cannot bear. . . .

"I am only Aldonza. I am no one! I'm nothing at all."

Yet in the end Aldonza accepts the Dulcinea within her and rises above her sordid origins. (*Man of La Mancha*, by Dale Wasserman, lyrics by Joe Darion, music by Mitch Leigh [New York: Random House, 1966], pp. 44–46.)

Had I not seen people rise up from such depths, this song would remain, for me, merely a dramatic part of a popular play. But it has been my privilege to see many Aldonzas arise, as well as many of their male counterparts. The journey was similar. First they began to dare to believe. Along the way they were hurt again; and they frequently lashed out in retaliation. Eventually they achieved a sense of self that overcame the downward pull of their past, and they concluded that they were worthy of respect; their own if not anyone else's. Thus they began to define themselves. Their guiding light was a hope in Christ and his infinite love.

You need not be a fallen Aldonza to hunger to define yourself. The righteous Nephi shared his struggle. Through intense introspection he seemed to grow ever more secure in his relationship with God. It was as if he defined himself once and for all as a servant of Christ. He began by wondering why he was so troubled, for, as he said,

> My soul delighteth in the things of the Lord; and my heart pondereth continually upon the things which I have seen and heard.

Then he recited his travail and his decision.

> Nevertheless, notwithstanding the great goodness of the Lord . . . my heart exclaimeth: O wretched man that I am! Yea, my heart sorroweth because of my flesh; my soul grieveth because of mine iniquities. . . .
>
> Nevertheless, I know in whom I have trusted. . . .
>
> And upon the wings of his Spirit hath my body been carried away upon exceedingly high mountains. And mine eyes have beheld great things. . . .
>
> O then, if I have seen so great things, if the Lord in his condescension unto the children of men hath visited men in so much mercy, why should my heart weep and my soul linger in the valley of sorrow . . . ?
>
> Rejoice, O my heart, and cry unto the Lord, and say: O Lord, I will praise thee forever; yea my soul will rejoice in thee, my God, and the rock of my salvation. (2 Nephi 4:16–17, 19, 25–26, 30.)

Throughout scripture we find accounts of the personal growth of heroic yet fallible men and women as they defined themselves through divine covenant relationships.

Eve and Adam, after a portentous transgression of a commandment, reaffirmed their fidelity to God, even though their hearts were wounded by Cain's murder of his good brother. We can picture them as their faces began to show the lines of parental anxiety, ennobled by unyielding fidelity to each other and to their covenants with God. They defined themselves, each in turn, by declaring their relationship to God. Adam said: "Blessed be the name of God, for because of my transgression my eyes are opened, and in this life I shall have joy, and again in the flesh I shall see God" (Moses 5:10).

To this mother Eve added her testament: "Were it not for our transgression we never should have had seed, and never should have known good and evil, and the joy of our redemption, and the eternal life which God giveth unto all the obedient" (Moses 5:11).

Abraham and Sarah defined themselves so firmly by a covenant relationship with God that they obeyed his command to conceive and bear a child although they were stricken in years. (Remember also that Abraham had suffered the painful experience of separating himself from his father as a result of rejecting his father's heathen traditions.)

Ruth grew from a naive bride to a widowed daughter-in-law and in the process gave us that sublime declaration of fidelity to an intimate relationship. In contrast to her sister-in-law, Ruth bound herself to her widowed mother-in-law. "Intreat me not to leave thee, or to return from following after thee: for whither thou goest, I will go; and where thou lodgest, I will lodge: thy people shall be my people, and thy God my God: where thou diest, will I die, and there will I be buried: the Lord do so to me, and more also, if ought but death part thee and me" (Ruth 1:16–17).

Peter, the man who had denied knowing the man Jesus, became the man who courageously acknowledged him throughout Palestine and beyond and died for his allegiance to the covenant he had made with his Redeemer.

In contrast, Jonah apparently had virtually no definition of himself. He was afraid not to obey God's command to go to Nineveh. He was afraid to offend the sailors. He was afraid of the sinners in Nineveh. He resented their repentance. It took a "great fish" to get his attention.

Summary

Job set a standard for self-definition as he resolutely maintained his integrity through horrific tests.

"As God liveth, who hath taken away my judgment; and the Almighty, who hath vexed my soul;

"All the while my breath is in me, and the spirit of God is in my nostrils;

"My lips shall not speak wickedness, nor my tongue utter deceit.

"God forbid that I should justify you: till I die I will not remove mine integrity from me.

"My righteousness I hold fast, and will not let it go: my heart shall not reproach me so long as I live." (Job 27:2–6.)

In the next three chapters we shall examine how to achieve self-definition by developing relationship skills, selecting values and traits, and gaining masculine or feminine security. Self-definition may encompass other elements too, but certainly these three have proven essential.

*Therefore, all things
whatsoever ye would that
men should do to you, do ye
even so to them, for this is
the law and the prophets.*
— 3 Nephi 14:12

Self-Definition: Development of Relationship Skills

CHAPTER FOUR

Good relationships do not happen by chance. They require thought and effort. By our own efforts we can enrich good relationships and heal troubled ones. There are definable, specific skills by which people can initiate and nurture relationships until they enjoy social and emotional intercourse in the finest sense of those terms.

Relationships can fit into three categories, which frequently develop into three phases: civil, affectionate, and intimate.

A civil relationship or the civil phase of a relationship is expected to be short-term, emotionally neutral or mild, with limited but formal physical contact; for example, courteous handshakes requiring little or no lasting commitment or feeling. Interaction with store clerks, other drivers on the road, people in an elevator, are usually in the civil category. These are numerous and of daily occurrence.

TELESTIAL TERRESTRIAL CELESTIAL

Society would grind to a halt without rules for civil interaction. Violence between drivers on busy public highways is just such a breakdown. Civil relationships, or this phase of a specific relationship, are expected to end. Indeed, failure to terminate can embarrass people. The sales clerk who is pleasant may become impatient if you try to visit with him at length, for he has other customers to serve in a role that requires civility *and* productivity.

In the civil phase of a relationship, use of the respectful titles "Mr.," "Mrs.," "Miss," "Sir," "Ma'am," is appropriate.

Excessive reliance on certain civilities instead of progressing to warmer interactions can reveal problems in relationships. A colleague of mine had spent months in trying to determine what relationship patterns were harming a certain family. Then he happened to be present when one of the family's teenage daughters received a special award that generated a fair amount of approving emotion among most people at the ceremony. When the daughter turned to seek her father's congratulations, he shook her hand and very obviously held her at arm's length.

Affectionate relationships are fewer in number and frequency than civil ones, but are longer lasting. People we enjoy enough to seek repeated contacts with, whom we might touch or speak to with warmth, whose leaving would sadden us, are included in our affectionate relationships. When these end, we experience a strong sense of loss. This phase within a specific relationship is intense. Words, thoughts, looks, and touches all have warmth, though they are not as ardent as those of intimacy. Neither are they as lukewarm as those of the civil kind. This phase of a relationship is too often missing from marriages. It is ironical and sad that many people go from civilities to sexual intimacies without affection. They "have sex" without affection, let alone without courtship and marriage.

Intimate relationships are powerful. They are also quite rare. They involve true intercourse, the intertwining of minds or hearts or bodies or all three in ways that go far beyond affection. Participants expose their innermost thoughts, open up their hearts, embrace. Such relationships are expected to endure over time and across distances. When they end, people grieve. The intimate phase of a relationship is intense, carrying within it seeds of surpassing commitment — and those of profound hostility if things should go awry.

Knowing of these three categories and practicing the skills they involve is a reliable way to define oneself. Relationships are enriched by proper attention to all three. After years of failure, people heal troubled relationships by earnest attention to the attitudes and activities needed for these categories. Refusal to develop the skills of all three phases will prevent the relationship from deepening as it should, or will perpetuate problems.

We will consider each of the three categories in some detail.

Civil Relationships

Mark would have benefitted from knowing and following James's counsel, "Wherefore, my beloved brethren, let every man be swift to hear, slow to speak" (James 1:19). Mark had an unfortunate wit and expressed it quicker than his mind could censor it. In some civil contacts he was adequate, in some unintentionally cruel. One day I observed him inflict pain on a custodial worker.

Mark (watching the man industriously vacuum the carpet): "Has anyone ever told you that you do very good work?"

Employee (with a hopeful smile, expecting a compliment for a thankless task): "No, sir. Thank you very much."

Mark (turning away too fast to catch the "Thank you very much"): "Well, think about it."

The employee's face fell as he realized he had been made to look a fool.

Confronted about this, Mark said that he had had no intention of hurting the man, that it was just his way of joking with people. But his way was so painful to others that his family was disintegrating.

After this episode Mark set out to practice being civil. He watched facial expressions and listened carefully. He mentally rehearsed civil contacts before he spoke. Soon he was reporting pleasant civil episodes almost daily. He also learned the difference between appropriate and inappropriate types of civil contact. To show appreciation to a store clerk who always gave him good service, one day Mark went on at some length about "how good you make me feel." The startled woman's reaction conveyed the obvious fear that Mark was seeking a sexual experience. Ruefully he concluded that there were limits to civil relationships.

Minimal civility at least lubricates ordinary social interaction. Benevolent civility elevates anyone who practices it and blesses those who are so treated. It is said that William Booth, founder of the Salvation Army, refused in 1868 to ever again celebrate a traditional Christmas with all the trappings because he was painfully aware that, as he ate sumptuously, the poor, especially the children, were starving.

Affectionate Relationships

Affectionate mannerisms are often subtle and require considerable skill. Touching is one example. Civil touching is rather formal, e.g., handshaking. Intimate touching is informal, e.g., holding hands. But in what manner does a person touch to express affection? Touching can be hand to hand or heart to heart. Simple neighborliness offers some of the finest ways: Food is taken to the family that just moved in next door. A house or apartment is watched while neighbors are away on vacation. Children are allowed to play in the safest yard so they can be off the busy street. Shopping is done for one who is too ill to get out. The list is as varied as are the kindnesses of which people are capable.

Because they are neither formal nor intense, affectionate relationships are often more difficult to imagine and practice than are civil or intimate relationships, but the results are well worth the effort.

A few paragraphs back we left Mark still learning in the area of civil relationships. He persisted in his efforts to acquire relationship skills. One success took place with his neighbors during a period when he was separated from his wife. He reported:

> Greg, my next-door neighbor, dropped by about 7:30 P.M., I guess, and asked me if I would like to come over to help decorate Easter eggs. So I told him that I would like that very much. The eggs were somewhat hot, but we managed to draw designs on them. I'm not very artistically inclined, but they were very kind in their remarks about the eggs I had colored. I thought some of them looked ghastly, but they thought they looked good! This made me feel good and led me on to higher and greater things.

When we were through making them all pretty colors, we stuck some glitter on some of them.

After the coloring I helped them clean up a bit, and at about 10:00 P.M. I went back to my place. It really felt good to associate with other people and have fun together.

Roy had been raised in a decidedly unaffectionate house, and at twenty-four years of age he could not even visualize how to express affection. To reach the point of being able to give and receive affection, he first ran through in his mind various experiences that were affectionate extensions of civility. Rehearsing a date, Roy imagined making the phone call. He reviewed what he might say, the young woman's possible responses, his reactions. Then he rehearsed how to greet her at her door and navigate her from the house to the car. Relatively confident due to these mental rehearsals, he ventured forth on an actual date, where he found to his great relief that he could handle well these civil preliminaries.

Becoming affectionate was more challenging. His values forbade resorting to alcohol or sexual activity. His friend with whom he rehearsed these forays, asked, "Tell me when and where you can touch the lady on the first, third, and fifth dates?" Roy drew a complete blank, so it was necessary for him to plan this strategically as if it were a military campaign.

Lest the reader be irritated by such a mechanical approach, remember that this young man had never seen his parents embrace, kiss, snuggle, or hold hands. Nor had he any memories of being touched by his father, and had few of being touched by his mother. Roy needed to learn the functions of affection in much the same way as someone else might learn how to swim or ride a bicycle.

At first Roy was awkward in these functions, and he had to rely on the basic rule of self-definition — never take yourself too seriously. Another basic rule is to set small goals and achieve them promptly. One especially practical goal Roy selected was participation in a church-group musical, where he gained confidence in an atmosphere of free expression. He was, as they say in show business, "a bit player," which made it possible for him to observe others in social and emotional situations, after which he would try his primitive skills. He literally created his own personal play within a play.

Was Roy unusual? Unfortunately he may represent a large segment of his generation, which, according to Allan Bloom, sees romance and courtship as woefully outmoded, not just because they seem old-fashioned but "because it would be offensive to women." (*The Closing of the American Mind* [New York: Simon and Schuster, 1987], pp. 116–17.)

It is necessary for children to see examples of parental civility and affection. When they do, as they negotiate their way through the turbulent passages of adolescence and young adulthood they know how decently and affectionately people can treat each other.

Here is Duane's own account of some affectionate times with his young son and namesake:

> Little Duane and I went to the bank to make a (small) deposit and everyone there was thrilled to see him and said how much he looks like me. (Good-looking fellow!) Then we went to the store and did a little shopping. . . . He likes to ride in the shopping carts and I like to push. Then we took the groceries to my place and we played on the floor for a while and looked out the window, etc. Then we decided to go for a walk with the stroller. He seemed to like this, and on the way back he went to sleep.
>
> Saturday we went to the lake and I took Duane paddling. He thought it was great fun and walked around in the water with me as I held his hands so he wouldn't fall over. At one point I let go of his hands and he just stood there on his own for about two minutes. He is learning to get his balance. He even took his first unaided walking step on Friday night.

Mark Twain observed a rough-hewn kind of affection between two old gold-miners in the Sierra Nevada mother lode country of the nineteenth century.

> I spent three months in the log-cabin home of Jim Gillis and his "pard," Dick Stoker, in Jackass Gulch, that serene and reposeful and dreamy and delicious sylvan paradise of which I have already spoken. Every now and then Jim would have an inspiration and he would stand up before the great log fire, with his back to it and his hands crossed behind him, and deliver himself of an elaborate impromptu lie—a fairy tale, an extravagant romance—with Dick Stoker as the hero of it as a general thing. Jim always soberly pretended that what he was relating was strictly history, veracious

history, not romance. Dick Stoker, gray-headed and good-natured, would sit smoking his pipe and listen with a gentle serenity to these monstrous fabrications and never utter a protest. (Mark Twain, *The Autobiography of Mark Twain* [New York: Washington Square Press, 1917], p. 152.)

Intimate Relationships

The term *intimacy* is so badly misused these days that discussion of intimacy first demands rejection of what it is not. *Intimacy* should no more be a synonym for *sexuality* than should *intercourse*. *Intimacy* is a word that ought to evoke in the mind and heart what even the dry dictionary defines in special terms: "Characterizing one's deepest nature; marked by a warm friendship developing through long association; informal warmth of a very personal, private nature."

Of course, sex has always been part of certain intimate relationships. We shall address it later as an enriching part of marriage. Marital relationships and values vary as widely as the human race, but what stands out as universal is that when time-tested and revealed rules for those relationships and values are abandoned, intimate relationships suffer. Where this occurs the basic social fabric tears and, unless it is mended, disintegrates. Many in this generation look back with amusement or scorn at what they characterize as old-fashioned and prudish but were actually sophisticated ways to be affectionate and intimate while remaining chaste — such as snuggling up on the porch swing, and holding hands but nothing more. We have lost such practices to our peril.

The current, impatient method is for two people to be superficially familiar before even knowing one another. Concurrently, conversation has become uninhibited among casual acquaintances or even strangers. For example, a popular talk show host gathered an audience of strangers in the studio with a panel of men who had overcome homosexuality and whose wives were present. In that setting, behavior that used to be an extremely private matter was discussed while thousands of viewers watched from their homes. No reciprocity was involved, no deepening of relationships. The duration was short. The panel and audience participants were unlikely ever to meet again. It was not an intimate experience. It was public disclosure of private behaviors.

What, then, are the thoughts, expressions, and actions of intimacy? We pray for our intimates. We write them loving letters. We attend to them during sickness. We rejoice in their achievements. We embrace and kiss them. We also may become angry and offended with them, for with intimacy there comes exceptional reward and exceptional risk. We forgive. We strive to maintain the relationship by telephone calls and planned reunions. We spend quiet times together, not feeling uncomfortable in the silence.

Lee Iacocca, the hard-charging automobile industry leader, told of his parents' ability to express intimacy:

"My parents were very open with their feelings and their love — not only at home, but also in public. Most of my friends would never hug their fathers. I guess they were afraid of not appearing strong and independent. But I hugged and kissed my dad at every opportunity — nothing could have felt more natural." (Lee Iacocca with William Novak, *Iacocca: An Autobiography* [New York: Bantam Books, 1984], p. 4.)

One strong woman who was struggling to recover from the ashes of a failed marriage wrote to an intimate female friend:

"How I miss you! However, all the qualities you demonstrate, all of the character traits you have and you've developed, bless me. Thinking of you calms my troubled heart — your memory washes over me with such love. . . .

"My blessings are great — immeasurable and beyond measure. My trials seem likewise. Lately I wonder how much the heart can bear. . . .

"Write if you can. My whole world [has] changed."

There are intimate relationships that do not, in fact must not, involve sexual behavior. They are no less powerful for it. The most obvious are those between parents and children. There are others too. One such is the incomparable English ice-dancing team of Jayne Torvill and Christopher Dean, who have been together for over ten years. They are partners in a sport that demands of performers more energy "in four minutes . . . than an ice hockey star [expends] in four 20-minute quarters."

Here are some excerpts from an article by Les Wilson about these two young, vigorous artist-athletes.

> One of the secrets of the couple's success, says Jayne, is not really a secret at all. It's the total commitment they give each other.
>
> Chris doesn't like carrying money, so on tour Jayne looks after the accounts and organizes the travel arrangements when their manager isn't around. On the other hand, he admits he'll open all the doors, fetch her tea, run her errands, and buy her an ice cream with their joint money if she's feeling a bit low. . . .
>
> Says Jayne: "I have a deep affection for Chris. I couldn't skate with him the way I do, pouring every emotion into it, if I didn't have that affection. And how could I spend most of my waking hours with someone if there wasn't a special situation?" . . .
>
> Jayne recalls vividly travelling home from their training ground some two years ago in Bavaria, for the first time on her *own*. She described it as an "eerie" experience. "I missed him — and not just to carry the bags," she admitted. . . .
>
> Some say the relationship is like marriage. "Perhaps, except that *we don't sleep together*," says Jayne, with not a blush in sight!
>
> Of the little fawn he throws around the ice rink, Chris Dean says he sees her in a "special" light. He believes, in a youthful way, that at the beginning they fell in love and then out of it and that was when they became the world-beating team.
>
> Chris says "Ours is a strange relationship. It's a mystery to most people — including ourselves!" . . .
>
> They know that a certain amount of friction at this level, living in each other's pockets, is almost inevitable. . . .
>
> Says Jayne: "We've been together for almost eight years and our relationship has to be more than just brother and sister. And yet we're not in love. I know it's hard to understand. One day, not yet though, we'll fall in love with other people; we'll live another life . . . dance that last dance together; I know it'll be an amazing and emotional moment." (Les Wilson, "Ice Pinnacle," *World of Sport,* July 1984, pp. 57–60.)

These two people have accomplished something in their rich intimacy that is so exceptional that many ice dancing experts believe it will never occur again. They speak of and they peerlessly demonstrate their civility, affection, and intimacy. Yet, as they are quoted as saying, as they have defined themselves there is not and cannot be the sexual contact that some would expect or even demand. The quality of their relationship reveals that discipline and constraints can actually increase the intensity of an intimate relationship.

In times of terrible distress we sometimes see revealed the noblest of intimate human relationships in those who define themselves as followers of Christ.

We noted earlier how Duane began to learn affection with his son, little Duane. There came a time when Duane had to write to his aged parents, who lived rather far away, and tell them of his serious marital and family problems. Had he mailed it, his first draft of the letter would have hurt them, for he portrayed himself as a helpless victim. With some coaching Duane rewrote the letter with his parents' needs in mind. Excerpts from their replies confirm both the correctness of the revision and the sublime heights to which the human heart can rise in the intimacy of generous love.

From Duane's father:

Thank you for your letter and the explanations contained therein. Naturally it is a great shock to us as we naturally thought that everything was fine with you all. . . .

I am glad that you thought very carefully what to write in your letter, we were both very upset, but the way that you very carefully worded the letter helped us to understand better the very traumatic and emotional experiences you have been going through.

It helped us a great deal when we telephoned you. . . . I wanted [Mother] to speak with you a good deal and clear the deep worry that was in her (both of us), I was afraid that she would have made herself very ill, hence I persuaded her that it would be best to phone you quickly.

What has happened, has happened, but I am sure that if you are prayerful, and sincerely try hard, you will overcome this tragic experience in your life.

You know how much we think of you, dear, and the great admiration we have for you, the way that you have stood on your own feet since you were sixteen. . . .

We love you so much, this is a testing time for you, but we know that you will pull through and that all will soon be well. God Bless, and do take care, we pray for you night and day, and we know that Heavenly Father will help.

Your Loving Dad.

From Duane's mother:

> I love you very much and feel so sorry for all that has happened. . . .
>
> The Lord loves you, and it seems to me he is watching over you. I believe you have a humble spirit and a contrite heart.
>
> Time is a great healer. If you think of anything you can do for [your wife and children] to make them happy, i.e., make something for them; send loving messages. Their response will bring your love which is bottled up out of you and you will feel [love] again. I cannot write what I mean very well but I do know that if first of all you do something because it is right, whether you feel like doing it or not, then in time you will do it because you want to and enjoy it and receive a great reward. Jesus said "Love one another as I have loved you," and one has to start somewhere.
>
> Do things for others that you know they will like, think of them first and forget your own unhappiness. There lies salvation.
>
> Make a practice of being kind to others, your rewards will be much more than you can imagine.

From the above excerpts one can appreciate the soothing balm with which these sublime parental reactions salved Duane's troubled mind. They personified one writer's definition of the quality of love expected of true Christians:

> The Christian ethic is an ethic of love. That love is not an easy-going, emotional, sentimental thing. It is not something subject to impulse and motivated by passion. It is not something which flames and then dies, at one time a burning passion, at another time almost non-existent. It is not something which depends on our likes and our dislikes for other people. It is the steady, unvarying, undefeatable determination to love men as Jesus loved them, and never, no matter what they do in response, to seek anything but their highest good. . . . This kind of love is going to have consequences. (William Barclay, *Ethics in a Permissive Society* [London: Harper and Row, 1971], p. 62.)

Alma wrote of this even more explicitly as he instructed his people about the ordinance and covenants of baptism:

> As ye are desirous to come into the fold of God, and to be called his people, and are willing to bear one another's burdens, that they may be light; yea, and are willing to mourn with those that

mourn; yea, and comfort those that stand in need of comfort, and to stand as witnesses of God at all times and in all things, and in all places that ye may be in, even until death. . . . If this be the desire of your hearts, what have you against being baptized in the name of the Lord, as a witness before him that ye have entered into a covenant with him, that ye will serve him and keep his commandments? (Mosiah 18:8–10.)

These words convey the duty of the believer. Within these same passages we find the loving promises from the Redeemer about obedience to these duties: "that ye may be redeemed of God, and be numbered with those of the first resurrection, that ye may have eternal life."

But the ultimate sense of intimacy is that experienced and often expressed by Christians past and present. It encompasses the great assurance — the wish, the hope, the knowledge that Jesus loves us in a way that no one else can. One woman I know who survived some of this world's worst relationship trials wrote in poetic form of her intimate relationship with her Savior.

> There is an intimate touch
>   in my life
> That even my husband
>   cannot give.
> I feel it when I get on
>   my knees in prayer,
> And know that my God
>   and Savior live.
> My insignificant soul is kissed
>   by one so much greater than me.
> Oh Lord, if only the veil would lift
>   that thy holiness I might see!

When sanctified by an eternal perspective, intimacy even eases the pain of death and transcends mortality. Willard Richards expressed this in his journal as his wife, Jennetta, lay dying in 1845:

The night before she died, she asked if Father and Mother was at home, and appeared rather bewildered for a few moments, as she seemed to arouse from a little rest. Although her head was generally clear and unusually free from pain during her sickness.

Her hair on the back of her head became somewhat matted, and it was cut, but the front remains entire. Jennetta had the best of watchers and nurses, most of them . . . women which seemed "like mothers" to her. . . .

I watched her thus closely not so much because I felt she was in danger as because I ever delighted to comfort and do her good, and it was always her delight to make me happy, and here you will pardon the remark, when I tell you we were one . . . and further . . . we saw each other in visions long before we met, and our course was marked for us in the Eternal world. . . . Death had no terrors for her; she knew in whom she had believed, and that he was able to save her. (Daughters of the Utah Pioneers, Lessons for November, 1959, pp. 134–35.)

Summary

There are three main types of human relationships. They can be labeled civil, affectionate, and intimate. A rich relationship can develop and progress through all three stages. Any relationship that lacks civility and affection is almost always harmful to at least one of the people involved. This particularly applies to sexual activity in which someone is being used merely to gratify appetite.

In defining ourselves it is essential that we learn and practice all three phases and types and thus develop effective skills. Diligence in addressing this aspect of self-definition makes it highly likely that relationships will deepen and grow.

Disciples of Christ have a divine example, one that was given through mortal relationships, one that teaches that relationships may be endlessly rich and that when pain and suffering strikes, it may be eased through perfect love.

*Remember faith, virtue,
knowledge, temperance,
patience, brotherly kind-
ness, godliness, charity,
humility, diligence. Ask,
and ye shall receive; knock,
and it shall be opened unto
you.*
—D&C 4:6–7

Self-Definition: Selecting Values and Traits

CHAPTER FIVE

Roy was so unsure of himself that in ordinary conversation he blushed, he shuffled his feet; his eyes wandered, and he spoke haltingly. The thought of giving a public speech terrified him. Lack of confidence affected every relationship he attempted, especially with women.

Roy wanted to become a contributing member of society; he valued participation and service. He knew he had to overcome his inhibitions. He began this process by selecting a person at church who he knew could carry on conversations and who gave talks in a confident, pleasant, calm manner. Roy observed these traits for a few weeks, thought about them, then at home began to practice them in front of a mirror. Within days his external mannerisms and internal emotions began to change; he began to speak with an outward confidence that reflected his growing inward confidence. His motivation for this change was the value he placed on becoming socially effective enough to help other people.

During infancy and childhood each of us forms the character traits that are blends of innate personality and our attempts to satisfy others' expectations of us. We tend to imitate our way into traits that affect relationships. Eventually we must ask ourselves whether our traits are in agreement with our values.

Few people have done this more openly or with more success than Benjamin Franklin, who set out on this course when, as he wryly noted, he "conceived the bold and arduous project of arriving at moral perfection." It was not long before he discovered that he had more faults than he had suspected. People who heal or enrich relationships are tolerant of their fellow strugglers and with themselves, for they soon yearn for mercy even as they are determined to improve.

The journey of self-definition ought to be exhilarating and uplifting. If it becomes sour and unpleasant, the traveler has taken a wrong turn. The acquisition of virtue and strength so enhances feelings about oneself that, as Franklin reported in his seventy-ninth year, "I was . . . a better and happier man than I otherwise should have been if I had not attempted it." Franklin recorded his efforts in his autobiography, from which the details can be gleaned.

His experience was simple. He listed the virtues he wished to develop, which included industry, sincerity, and frugality. He wrote down a brief, one-sentence description of the virtue as he intended to live it. He divided the notebook into days and weeks. At the end of each day he marked his progress, concentrating on one virtue for one week, then shifting the focus to another virtue, and so on. As the days rolled into weeks and the weeks into months, Franklin had evidence on paper to reinforce the feelings he had about his behavioral and relationship improvements. With this almost primitive tool a young man whose family relationships had been painful refined himself into one of the most widely respected men in the world. But, more important to the matters we are examining, he defined himself precisely and acquired traits after thoroughly considering many possible values.

Franklin is not alone in such an organized program of acquiring virtues. Many people have set out on such courses with equally benevolent results. Elder Marion G. Romney, Apostle and member of the First Presidency, adopted a similar regimen, although with much more spiritual emphasis. His lists were headed: Relationship to the Lord; Activities Within the Church; Relationship with Others; and Personal Conduct.

Under "Activities Within the Church," among the virtues listed by Elder Romney were:

— Receive the words of the President of the Church as if they were spoken by the Lord God himself.
— Meet together often to partake of the sacrament.
— Teach one another the doctrine of the kingdom.
— Seek diligently to turn the hearts of the children to their fathers, and the hearts of the fathers to their children.
— Pay tithing.
— Consecrate of thy properties [for the] support of the poor.
— Arise and shine forth, that thy light may be a standard for all nations.

Under "Personal Conduct," he listed:

— Live not after the manner of the world.
— Be diligent.
— Seek learning, even by study and also by faith.
— Thou shalt not be idle.
— Be thrifty.
— Be anxiously engaged in a good cause.
— Cease to sleep longer than is needful.
— Arise early and retire to thy bed early.
— Abstain from the use of wine, tobacco, strong and hot drinks.
— Eat meat sparingly.
— Remember wheat for man.
— Do not covet. Do not boast.
— Beware of pride.
— Seek not the praise of the world.
— Be meek and humble.
— Observe the Sabbath day to keep it holy.
— Purify your hearts and cleanse your hands.
— Cast away your idle thoughts and your excess laughter.
— Cease to be unclean.

— Practice virtue and holiness . . . continually.
— Live by every word that proceedeth forth from the mouth of God.
—Be faithful unto death.
   (F. Burton Howard, *Marion G. Romney* [Salt Lake City: Bookcraft, 1988], pp. 188–90.)

Selecting values and traits such as did Benjamin Franklin and Elder Romney is a necessary part of self-definition. No one who is serious about relationships can avoid it.

As he applied this practice of selecting values and traits, Leon was well aware that his enthusiasm was often mistaken for aggression. As a consequence, family members and co-workers were intimidated by him, even when he was trying to reassure them. For his part, Leon, noticing that a certain colleague's manner seemed to reassure people, found himself envying that person even though his ideas often conflicted with Leon's. Observing the colleague more closely, Leon noted that he did not speak often, and when he did it was quietly, calmly. To Leon he actually seemed aloof. Nevertheless, Leon decided to emulate the cooler trait, up to a point. From another man Leon selected a trait of asking questions rather than making declarations, especially when sensitive issues were involved.

As Leon sought to make these two traits his own, they seemed artificial and uncomfortable at first. They slowed things down, or, more accurately, they slowed down Leon's impassioned speech habits. But after several weeks he began to see results. People who formerly had avoided any discussion with him actually sought him out. Now tensions seldom arose, even during discussion of difficult matters. And he stumbled on to a fascinating fact that applied most of the time: Inevitably someone else asked the questions or made the comments he had formerly burned to express; or, if the precise question was not asked, he could ease the discussion toward it by a mild inquiry or two. Emotions still flared within his heart and mind, but he actually made more progress by using this calmer way. There were times when integrity demanded a firm statement of principle, to be sure, but even these assertions had become less aggressive and more palatable to those with whom he was disagreeing.

Besides their selection and adoption, clarification of values and traits can enhance relationships. Bruce was intense, his wife was relaxed. Bruce was critical of virtually everything his wife did. His incessant nagging upset their relationship to the point that they sought professional counseling. It transpired that Bruce admired his wife greatly and wanted to improve the relationship, not harm it. He came to recognize that his criticism was not so much about her alleged weaknesses as about her less intense approach to life. Eventually he saw that her way would probably never lead to colitis, as had his. As Bruce observed more carefully his wife's characteristic of the relaxed approach, he made an important discovery: she actually took his comments seriously — *the first time*. The second and third attack of criticism forced her to either defend herself or withdraw. He also noticed that she had a way of telling him things once. After that she never commented on those matters while they were angry, unless he had pushed her beyond her limits; and even then she steadied down rather quickly, though he remained agitated.

Because he felt a fool after he had berated someone he loved, and because he knew his approach was harming their relationship, Bruce began to imitate his wife's trait. To preserve his male dignity he practiced outside the home for some time, so that his wife would not notice this. Eventually, though, he became so comfortable with the trait that he automatically began to use it in the home. The result was as oil poured on troubled waters. Though it was occasionally disrupted by the normal pressures of living, a calm came into the family as a soothing spirit developed.

Adopting certain selected values and traits is also effective when a person needs to learn how to expect *others* to behave. Sad to say, this is necessary for victims of child abuse, who must actually see non-abusing, nurturing behavior as part of their healing. If they see it they can hope for it for themselves and learn to trust again.

As a child, Nancy had been abused by her parents — sexually by her father, with beatings by her mother. She left home as soon as someone would provide her with shelter, and at sixteen she married a man who eventually abused her. He also abused their children. She divorced her husband and set about rebuilding her family of four. Thereafter it wasn't so much bitterness toward men that hampered her relationship efforts as it was her doubt that any of them could be trusted. In her doubts she began to teach her daughters to defend themselves against men, and her boys to be apologetic for being male.

To urge Nancy to look for an ideal man would have compounded the problem, for such does not exist. It was possible, though, for her to observe closely some men who had kindly values and traits. One was her employer. He was patient and gentle, consistently showing respect for women. Over a two-year period she became convinced that such behavior existed.

Another man was a fellow church member. His often stern demeanor occasionally reminded her of her father, but in his unfailing solicitude he bore no resemblance to the man who had violated her.

Over time, Nancy began to expect that some men had traits that merited trust.

Summary

Values, as stated earlier, are those beliefs we act upon and turn into traits. Benjamin Franklin put this in perspective. His neighbor, a blacksmith, was approached by a man who wanted to buy at a favorable price an ax that was dull and speckled with rust. As a part of the sale the buyer required that the smith polish the ax so that the whole head was as bright and unspeckled as the cutting edge. The smith readily agreed, but he needed his customer to turn the sharpening stone. As Franklin narrates it, the customer turned the wheel "while the smith pressed the broad face of the ax hard and heavily on the stone, which made the turning of it very fatiguing." The customer stopped turning every now and then to see how the ax was progressing. After a while he wearily said he would take the ax as it was, speckled and all. " 'No,' said the smith, 'turn on, turn on; we shall have it bright by-and-by; as yet, it is only speckled.' 'Yes,' says the man, *'but I think I like a speckled ax best.'* " (*The Autobiography of Benjamin Franklin* [New York: Washington Square Press, 1955], pp. 109–10; italics in original.)

The people who enrich or heal relationships decide what they believe about relationships and then act upon those beliefs. The assumption made here, of course, is that the reader will select the appropriate values and then act on them, not to achieve some self-righteous superiority over others but to turn them into good and decent character traits.

Self-Definition:
Gaining Masculine or
Feminine Security

CHAPTER SIX

One day while waiting for my car at the garage I watched various male employees as they dealt with customers. One woman customer was obviously confused about things mechanical. I wondered what would be the employees' reaction to a man who seemed as confused. And what would that customer's feelings be if he could not speak garage lingo?

What is the first question asked about every newborn baby? "Is it a boy or a girl?" And thereafter an enormous weight of expectations bears down upon that person. The ability to define ourselves by those expectations determines much about our future relationships. For the rest of a man's life he is influenced by the fraternity of other men, as a woman is by her gender sorority. Admittance to the fraternity or sorority is automatic at first, but as the years go by we feel that we must prove ourselves to the official and unofficial arbiters of membership. There are countless tests. If we fail we may not be accepted, or so we fear.

These fears concerning masculinity and femininity are classic examples of the need for self-definition. Each of us must decide what kind of man or woman he or she *chooses* to be. If our sole reference point is the fraternity or sorority we are immediately at risk, for the rules change constantly. This is why we quote first at the beginning of this chapter the Savior's admonition that it is he who is the true exemplar of manhood — and, by proper extension, of womanhood. To seek to emulate him in every way, though this is an almost overwhelming project, also enables a person to enrich or heal relationships. He is, after all, the only historical figure who asked people to emulate him in every thought and deed.

Men who are unsure of their masculinity and adopt crude, ugly definitions for it have difficulty in relating to anyone, whether male or female, adult or child. Rape or incest may be committed by men who feel inadequate with *men*. It is well established that rape is a crime of violence and not of sex. Incest by a father upon a daughter often has more to do with his fears about masculinity than his inability to perform sexually with adult women. Thus it often happens that the mother of an incest victim will report: "Our sex life was all right. Why did he need a child?"

The following is taken from the business card of a forty-year-old who defined himself as a soldier of fortune: "Philanthropist, hero of the oppressed, casual hero, world traveler, wars fought, revolutions started, assassinations plotted, governments run, uprisings quelled, tigers tamed, bars emptied." The man who owned the card meant these expressions in all seriousness. He assiduously cultivated an image of machismo, and he maintained mistresses in various parts of the world. Yet at the same time he sexually abused his children, boys and girls. Those men who knew him well found him uncomfortable to be around. On one occasion he practically ran away from a family gathering when mildly confronted by another man. At a wedding reception virtually no one conversed with him, even though only three people there knew of his crimes against his children. There was an invisible but real barrier that kept him out of social interaction with most other men. His father wrote him letters in language appropriate for chiding a youngster. Even in the military and quasi-military lives he led he was not included in easy-going camaraderie.

This is an extreme case of a syndrome that affects many men. If they cannot feel securely masculine, they fail to establish healthy relationships. Or, desperate to gain admittance to the fraternity, they do whatever they hope will open the door. Hence there are men who will spend undue time at the workplace, at play, or even at church, not because of love for the activity but because they seek acceptance by other men who hold male power.

The more secure a man (or boy) is in his masculinity, the less he feels obligated to assert himself over others, especially women. The secure man often is gentle and unassuming, for he is not driven to prove that he belongs to the fraternity. In fact, knowing what the fraternity is like from the inside, he is not very impressed with it anyway, for he knows how ridiculous many of the fraternity practices are. And that of course is true of some practices in the sorority.

Robert's lack of confidence in relating to other adults was so severe that for the greater part of his life he had restricted himself to necessary business and church contacts. There was virtually no social and emotional enjoyment in his life. As he undertook to correct this situation by the effort of defining himself, building masculine security was a major step. He began to achieve it by learning and performing a few skills that the fraternity considers masculine. He recorded several of them in his journal:

> Yesterday I got up fairly early, ran about 5 miles, came back and did calisthenics . . . went wind-surfing for a couple of hours . . . paid a quick visit to one of my soccer players (somehow I'm trying to coach soccer again this year). . . . Today was an easy day. Ran about 6 miles this morning, then came home and mowed the lawn. Coached a soccer game at 11:30, then brought the boys over here for a barbecue and swim party. . . . I feel better than I ever have in my life. Probably the main reason is that [my wife] is expecting again. . . . We are sure excited and are praying for the best this time. . . . I've also taken off quite a bit of weight, down to 162, have had all of my clothes taken in for about a year now. . . . I'm running a lot . . . and love every minute of it. I've just had a complete physical, and the doctor says I'm in perfect health — even have perfect blood pressure, which surprised me, as I feel like I live under quite a bit of stress, from my personal schedule.

Robert's self-definition did not spring from machismo or chauvinism. Rather, he deliberately gained enough gender security to be his own version of an adequate male, with some regard for the fraternity's expectations. Beyond these he became nurturant, physically strong, gentle, a kind listener, a hard worker.

The process is similar for women. In an age of militant feminism an emotional advantage accruing to women has been overlooked. The female sorority grants its members greater emotional and social range than does the male fraternity. Any rational person knows that a *real* man can enjoy growing flowers or doing needlepoint. Or that a *real* woman can play basketball or hammer a nail. A rational person knows just as well that if that same man cannot discuss football or automobiles with some familiarity his masculinity will be suspect, as will the woman's femininity if she never puts on a dress or cooks a meal. If this man does talk of football, or has played it, and the woman occasionally dons an apron and cooks, their masculinity or femininity are well enough established that others will allow them room to be "themselves."

A very straightforward method of achieving minimal gender security is to develop basic skills in one or two traditionally gender-related activities. It is a most practical step to prove to oneself and others that a fellow can throw a ball or jog or fish or that a woman can bake bread or sew. Then, having satisfied the requirements of the fraternity or the sorority, the man or woman can go and create his or her own unique version of self. This can enhance or even heal relationships which have been affected by perceived gender inadequacy.

Heber J. Grant (1856–1945), seventh President of The Church of Jesus Christ of Latter-day Saints, left fatherless at nine days of age, was raised as an only child by his devoted mother. Inevitably he learned more household skills than boys' pastimes. At age nine he joined the neighborhood ball games but was relegated to play with the very youngest boys because he lacked both the skills and the strength to run, throw, or bat well. He recalled in later years "when [he] picked up a ball, the boys would generally shout, 'Throw it here, sissy!' " It was in response to these taunts that Heber "solemnly vowed that [he] would play baseball in the nine that would win the championship of the Territory of Utah." After many long sessions of arduous practice in throwing baseballs he "played in the nine that won the championship of the Territory." He added, "Having thus made good my promise to myself, I retired from the baseball arena." (Preston Nibley, *The Presidents of the Church* [Salt Lake City: Deseret Book Company, 1959], pp. 274–75.)

In addition to defining himself by a basic male skill, Heber went on to expand his self-definition by developing a lifelong relationship with Jesus Christ.

From this sublime example we turn to darker instances of how uncertainty about one's gender security can be devastating. Leon discovered his insecurity when at about age fourteen he dressed up as a girl for Halloween. Years later he readily remembered why it was so upsetting. As a young boy he felt awkward, unattractive, and unpopular. When he looked in the mirror that Halloween night he felt pretty, someone who might be desirable to others. His reaction was immediately to remove his makeup and costume. Never again was he able to put on any kind of costume.

Benny had a more traumatic experience. A lonely and insecure boy, he dressed in his sister's clothes on occasion. One evening he was out for a drive when his car stalled. An acquaintance who stopped to help discovered the masquerade and spread the tale through the small town. As a consequence Benny was cruelly derided.

There are significant comparisons to make between Leon and Benny. They both pursued male, even macho, activities throughout their adolescent years. But their motives were crucially different. Leon sought admittance to the fraternity. Benny wanted to get out. Eventually Leon accepted himself as a gentler, less aggressive, but quite acceptable male. Benny tried to become a female, with terrible consequences until he realized that all along he could have opted to be the kind of man he preferred to be, that there are virtually no limits to the decent variations of masculinity and femininity. Erik Erikson spoke of this when asked how the task of forming psychosexual identities differs as between boys and girls.

> The task itself doesn't differ; the main stages, strengths, and risks do not differ for men and for women. Rather, they help sexual differences to complement one another. Children do have to

learn to become boys and girls, but unless there is very strong sex-typing going on, both sexes have a certain freedom. . . . It all depends on what the culture makes of it. But essentially, whatever strength has to develop in a certain stage must appear in both boys and girls. Like willpower, or industry. Or identity. (Elizabeth Hall, "A Conversation with Erik Erikson," *Psychology Today*, June 1983, pp. 27–28.)

Ancient Judeo-Christian values, modern scripture, and priesthood covenants surrounding them have bearing here. They call for clear gender distinctions. For example, the Hebrews were under injunction not to cross dress. "The woman shall not wear that which pertaineth unto a man, neither shall a man put on a woman's garment: for all that do so are abomination unto the Lord thy God" (Deuteronomy 22:5).

Grevious mischief has been done in the effort to erase distinctions between men and women. Just as grevious mischief is done in trying to coerce any woman or man into an emotional mold that is too confining for the growth of that individual human being. An interesting essay was written by a mother who was working on her Ph.D. in philosophy of mathematics. Her name is Margarita R. Levin. Here are a few extracts.

> *Who Are the People in Your Neighborhood* the book was called. Hmm, I wondered, would this be a good book for my little son? Opening it, I found Ms. Mail Carrier delivering letters and seeing all the people in the neighborhood: Ms. Auto Mechanic, Ms. Traffic Cop, Ms. Doctor and Ms. Telephone Repairer. Mr. Fireman and Mr. Grocer were there too, but almost none of the women were doing anything "traditional." Clearly, the "neighborhood" of the title was Libland, where all feminist wishes came true. . . .
>
> All this is wonderful if you're Marlo Thomas or Alan Alda, and you want your children to be dutiful citizens of Libland. But what about the rest of us who want our children to learn about the world as it really is? . . .
>
> The current flow of "liberated" books is due largely to publishers' "guidelines for non-sexist writing," which in turn resulted from pressure brought by a small group of dedicated feminists, few of whom have children of their own. Angry letters and general carrying-on by these extremists were not countered by any de-

fense of tradition, since those of us who were satisfied with the status quo didn't think we held a "position" in need of defending. We approved of having a few female doctors and fathers shown playing with their children, since such examples would be true to life. But the portrayal of women in these latest books is completely distorted: lots of bricklayers and lawyers but few, if any, mothers with their children. . . .

Let me venture even further by suggesting that there just may be some truth in those "stereotypes" about neat girls and fiesty boys. Psychology is proving harder to rewrite than alphabet books. Libland is not real and never will be so long as boys are boys and girls are girls. . . .

If we don't speak up now, our children may find themselves confronted with Long Jane Silver and a Wendy who fights Captain Hook while Peter Pan stays home to care for the boys. (Margarita R. Levin, "Babes in Libland," *Newsweek*, 28 December 1981, p. 8.)

Betty Friedan, a matriarch of feminism, had the integrity to evaluate these issues in her book *The Second Stage*. Her retrospection deals with the essence of female and male security. She writes:

I sense something off, out of focus, going wrong, in the terms by which [women today] are trying to live the equality we fought for. . . .

Around 1969, when that anti-man, anti-family, bra-burning image of "women's lib" was built up in [news] stories . . . I remember the helpless feeling . . . "But that's not what we meant, not at all." For us, with our roots in the middle American mainstream and our own fifties' families, equality and the personhood of women never meant destruction of the family, repudiation of marriage and motherhood, or implacable sexual war against men. (*The Second Stage* [New York: Summit Books, 1981], pp. 15, 47.)

Mrs. Friedan and Mrs. Levin recognized the grave risk in which women and men are placed if all vestiges of time-tested gender-based values should be wiped out. All that would be left would be a struggle for power. This is also known as survival of the fittest or social Darwinism.

Malachi's ominous warning rings down through two millennia to those who would ignore God's expectations of men who hold his priesthood. "Remember ye the law of Moses my servant, which I commanded unto him in Horeb for all Israel, with the statutes and judgments. Behold, I will send you Elijah the prophet before the coming of the great and dreadful day of the Lord: and he shall turn the heart of the fathers to the children, and the heart of the children to their fathers, lest I come and smite the earth with a curse." (Malachi 4:4-6.)

Aren't we seeing a curse as families disintegrate when fathers abandon their wives and children? Women then are left desolate to struggle in loneliness, bereft of the protection of their natural protectors — in the best case honorable, priesthood patriarchs filling the true masculine role.

Represented by "our glorious Mother Eve with many of her faithful daughters [women have] lived through the ages and worshiped the true and living God" (D&C 138:39). When husbands have failed their righteous wives the latter's cries for help have been heard by a concerned Father: "Ye have broken the hearts of your tender wives, and lost the confidence of your children, because of your bad examples before them; and the sobbings of their hearts ascend up to God against you" (Jacob 2:35).

In our day even the hearts of some women are turning cold as they define themselves into self-focus and away from nurturance. Other women are shocked into insensitivity by what has been lost from the definition of womanhood. Mrs. Friedan reported a friend's sad experience: "An ambitious woman journalist of my acquaintance, a fervent feminist, was forced to take to her bed for six months by some mysterious joint disease that may or may not have been related to her rather extreme 'workaholic' obsession. But even she was shocked when a 'workaholic' woman friend and neighbor was 'too busy' to stop off and buy her a carton of milk on her way home from work. She now blames feminism for the loss of the traditional 'caring' that women had for women, as well as for men and children." (*The Second Stage*, pp. 21-22.)

But let us not conclude the chapter on such a sad note. May I suggest that you engage in some immediate research. Review in your mind the men and women you know who represent the finest in masculinity or femininity. Not those who dress in the latest fashion, not those who dominate everyone around them, not those who loudly and frequently proclaim their own efforts to fit a stereotype. Rather, review those men and women who are so secure in their respective masculinity or femininity that they are unassumingly, modestly, quietly, Christlike in their behavior.

Robert, of whose masculine self-definition we read a few pages earlier, did just this. He observed a man we will refer to as Brother Jones. Brother Jones held a prominent priesthood calling. He was successful in his profession and talented in various ways. But Robert's admiration was directed at Brother Jones's tenderness with his children and with his wife. Robert noted how Brother Jones regularly took each of the children out individually. Robert saw that Brother Jones embraced his children and kissed them. He watched Brother Jones open doors for Sister Jones and take her arm to protect her against a stumble. He knew that Brother Jones knelt in prayer with his loved ones. And Brother Jones, so far as Robert knew, used the same clean language at work as he did at home.

Was Brother Jones perfect? Hardly, as he no doubt would be the first to point out. But what Robert knew was that this man was humbly yet powerfully secure in his masculinity. And by his security he created a climate in which his children and his wife could be secure. By his own stability he enhanced all of their relationships, as well as Robert's. And when the inevitable trials occurred with some of his children, he was able to heal relationships with a sureness that is missing in the insecure man, for he could give of himself rather than be obliged to require the child to conform to the father's need to be reassured.

Summary

It would be a woeful error for the reader to misinterpret this chapter as a diatribe against the urgent needs of some women to break free of oppression. Nor is it a proposal that men become effeminate. Militant feminism would not exist had there not been centuries of oppressive traditions that bore down heavily on certain women. There would be fewer sexually confused men had their gender roles included gentleness. And if these circumstances had obtained, relationships between the two sexes would not now be so stormy.

In basic biologic, cultural, and religious ways men are men and women are women, and for appropriate self-definition each needs to feel secure within his or her gender so as to enter into and maintain enjoyable, enduring relationships. This involves learning and doing a few simple things that settle a person into a basic sense of gender security. Once this is accomplished, the individual can define and discipline himself or herself to become unique. The model for that uniqueness is a crucial choice, Jesus Christ being the only completely reliable such model.

Self-definition has been described in three phases: development of relationship skills, selecting virtuous values and traits, and gaining masculine or feminine security. By attending to each of these a person learns what to expect of himself, what to expect of others, and what others may reasonably or even righteously expect of him in the effort to heal or otherwise enhance relationships.

And every man that striveth
for the mastery is temperate
in all things.
— 1 Corinthians 9:25

Self-Discipline

CHAPTER SEVEN

Without self-discipline, self-definition — discussed in the previous four chapters — could be merely an intellectual exercise. Some of the most influential philosophers and writers over the years have eloquently striven to define themselves yet from lack of self-discipline have failed miserably in relationships; Charles Dickens, Jean-Jacques Rousseau, and Leo Tolstoy, to name a few.

As we are using the term here, *self-discipline* means the process by which a person learns how to set value-based goals and works to achieve them. Such achievements require no one else's collaboration or approval. They are internal. They are self-directed. Each victory in the process leads to another, until the person is, as far as is feasible, in control of his or her life. But as Paul said, it is "temperate" mastery. It is not over-zealous, selfish, or unkind, for to be so would wound relationships, not enrich or heal them.

It seems ironical, but an enemy of relationships is unrestrained passion. Alma counseled his son Shiblon about passion and love:

"See that ye bridle all your passions, that ye may be filled with love" (Alma 38:12). By working to gain self-discipline we can invest our emotions wisely, warmly, and to the benefit of others. Without such discipline many people will use others to satisfy their own needs. At best this is unkind. At worst it is abusive.

At the state fair my wife and I watched a remarkable horse-training feat. The trainer, an older man, began with an unbroken mare. The spirited dapple-gray animal had never been ridden, and at first she ran around the corral trying to evade the trainer. For more than one and a half hours, without inflicting punishment or pain, the trainer taught the mare to come up to him and accept the saddle. Finally he rode her. She responded to his every wish. She trotted, cantered, stopped, backed up, turned right or left. Not once did she buck or shiver as if to rid herself of the rider. All this occurred without the trainer putting on the horse a bridle, a bit, or even a halter. In other words, in about two hours the mare progressed from fear and rebellion (the trainer's words) to trust and obedience.

The most impressive part of the demonstration was the trainer. Before he was through he was soaked with sweat. But he never raised his voice. The lariat was used to teach, not to hurt. As he said frequently, his aim was to reward the horse for doing what was right, not to punish her for misbehaving. The greatest lesson taught that day was by an old cowboy who stomped around a dusty corral, sharing his philosophy in rugged grammar, not once losing his calm, skilled, intelligent, disciplined mastery of the situation.

The cowboy's self-control and his treatment of the horse can be used as an analogy to what James spoke of as regards human relationships and self-discipline:

> For in many things we offend all. If any man offend not in word, the same is a perfect man, and able also to bridle the whole body.
>
> Behold, we put bits in the horses' mouths, that they may obey us; and we turn about their whole body.
>
> Behold also the ships, which though they be so great, and are driven of fierce winds, yet are they turned about with a very small helm, withersoever the governor listeth.

Even so the tongue is a little member, and boasteth great things. Behold, how great a matter a little fire kindleth.

For where envying and strife is, there is confusion and every evil work.

But the wisdom that is from above is first pure, then peaceable, gentle, and easy to be intreated, full of mercy and good fruits, without partiality, and without hypocrisy.

And the fruit of righteousness is sown in peace of them that make peace. (James 3:2-5, 16-18.)

Self-discipline is a joyous experience. There is no comparison between its product and that of self-indulgence. After a self-indulgent episode a normal person feels weak and demeaned, ashamed and regretful. After an exercise in self-discipline just the opposite emotions reinforce self-esteem.

Self-discipline is different from self-mastery. Does anyone ever master himself, at least in this life? There always exists the temptation, the thorn in one's flesh, the recognition that in the right (or wrong) circumstances one could — or at least might — falter. Paul the Apostle, a highly disciplined person, described this situation candidly:

And lest I should be exalted above measure through the abundance of the revelations, there was given to me a thorn in the flesh, the messenger of Satan to buffet me, lest I should be exalted above measure.

For this thing I besought the Lord thrice, that it might depart from me.

And he said unto me, My grace is sufficient for thee: for my strength is made perfect in weakness. Most gladly therefore will I rather glory in my infirmities, that the power of Christ may rest upon me.

Therefore I take pleasure in infirmities, in reproaches, in necessities, in persecutions, in distresses for Christ's sake: for when I am weak, then am I strong. (2 Corinthians 12:7-10.)

Paul attributes his hope to the only person who ever claimed total self-mastery — Jesus Christ, who said, "I have overcome the world" (John 16:33). (This is another reason why we must view Jesus as either who he claimed to be or as a total fraud.)

It seems realistic, then, to speak of discipline rather than of mastery. This is certainly a more accurate description of the controls developed by people who have enriched or healed relationships.

There are differences too between self-discipline and its various counterfeits, ascetic self-denial being one. The various forms of self-infliction range from eating disorders such as anorexia and bulimia to desire for physical and emotional pain. And, of course, there are individuals who careen from indulgence to indulgence.

Here history, values, observation, and religion serve us well. We examine the human family and ask ourselves whether self-discipline is worth the effort; or whether it has become obsolete in the modern era. The very attempt to justify achieving control of one's emotions and behavior seems strange when one reflects that only a few years ago every normal adult would have agreed that *a* mark, if not *the* mark, of maturity was self-discipline. A basic doctrine of psychology used to be that it was a mature trait to be able to defer gratification; and this deferment led to virtues such as saving money instead of squandering it, staying in school until graduation, controlling one's temper, and remaining virginal until marriage. Since then, however, a few decades of theories and amoral experiments in the field of human relationships have blinded many people to the crucial importance of self-discipline; and these theories and experiments defy the evidence of thousands of years of human history and hundreds if not thousands of human cultures wherein control of emotion and behavior has been the foundation of orderly society.

One young mother with Job-like integrity wrote to a friend after her husband had deserted her and her young children:

> Peace of mind is the thing I have of greatest value. It is my priceless pearl. Without it I am nothing—without it I cannot cope. Without it I will fail-falter. It encompasses dignity, good self-image, and personal power. The way of rewards for the right are so long-range. No promises are given for all of mortality. I think of that as little as possible. I try to live one day only.

Several years later, after having been true to her values and her covenants with God, she wrote with a certitude that is earned through integrity:

Things are really working out better than they logically should, especially financially. At first I thought every month that we'd drown in the tidal wave, but now I've come to see that somehow we don't, and I even count on surviving it and thank the Lord continually for enhancing our abilities and whatever else He does to make things work out. We are indebted to God, Jesus, and the Holy Ghost. They help us every day—we really are so minute, miniscule, as nothing without them. We are grateful for health and talents, and work very diligently to improve, but without God we just can't meet the power of the Earth.

Nephi expressed similar sentiments.

O Lord, I have trusted in thee, and I will trust in thee forever. I will not put my trust in the arm of flesh; for I know that cursed is he that putteth his trust in the arm of flesh. Yea, cursed is he that putteth his trust in man or maketh flesh his arm.

Yea, I know that God will give liberally to him that asketh. Yea, my God will give me, if I ask not amiss; therefore I will lift up my voice unto thee . . . my God, the rock of my righteousness. Behold, my voice shall forever ascend up unto thee, my rock and mine everlasting God. (2 Nephi 4:34–35.)

The work of self-discipline is a strength woven into the fabric of self-definition. With it, that fabric is strong and resilient. Without it, the fabric eventually, inevitably, tears; although fortunately it may be mended.

How often we see people who persevere through the trials of life because they are self-disciplined!

To set a goal and reach it gives us undeniable evidence of our strength, whatever others might think. As long as we are unduly influenced by criticism, by flattery, or by dependence we are not in control of our relationships. It is foolish to believe all that either our critics or our flatterers say.

The response of one marriage counselor to a forlorn husband comes to mind. Told by his wife to "Go to hell," the husband inquired of the counselor how he should respond. The counselor urged him not to go. On the other hand, the only reason why the fabled emperor was persuaded to parade unclothed in front of his fascinated subjects was that he relied on others to assure him that he was without flaw. Self-discipline lies somewhere between not going where we are told to and not believing what certain foolish people would whisper in our eager ears.

Consider a few of the many proven exercises by which we can develop self-discipline.

Inventorying Strengths and Weaknesses

From chapter 5 you will recall Benjamin Franklin's classic example on selecting values and traits. He simply listed his strengths and weaknesses and then set about refining the former and changing the latter. In this exercise we can learn from the woman in a comic strip:

Husband: "Do you realize it's New Year's Eve tomorrow?"

Wife: "I know."

Husband: "Are you going to make any New Year's resolutions this year?"

Wife: "I'm going to resolve not to smoke."

Husband: "But you've never smoked."

Wife: "And I resolve not to next year either. What's wrong with that?"

Husband: "Are you saying that you're going to resolve not to do something you're already not doing?"

Wife: "Exactly. It's taken me many years, but I've finally got the hang of this New Year's resolution business."

Few of us have difficulty in listing our weaknesses. To list strengths is usually harder. We do not always see our good points —we *hope* we have some, we *feel* we have some, but modesty prevents us from admitting them; or we fear that if we state them, someone will disapprove. Nevertheless it is essential that these lists originate with and be controlled by ourselves and not be extracted from others. To do otherwise would negate *self*-definition.

First, then, write down your strengths and weaknesses. These will probably be traits about which you have strong values. Here are two edited lists, the first from a man and the second from a woman.

The Man's List

Strengths	Weaknesses

Strengths

1. Love wife and children
2. Like people
3. Empathic
4. Strong willed
5. Loyal
6. Good morals and thoughts and feelings
7. Help others
8. Make friends easily
9. Hard worker
10. Good friend with God
11. Make decisions easily
12. Enjoy culture
13. Courageous

Weaknesses

1. Feelings hurt easily
2. Make cutting remarks
3. Stubborn
4. Jealous
5. Speak in a loud voice instead of soft
6. Hard time facing past
7. Can't forgive self easily
8. Overreact

The Woman's List

Strengths

1. Love children
2. Generous
3. Quiet
4. Don't panic
5. Helpful
6. Like to use hands
7. Like to read
8. Like cultural arts

Weaknesses

1. Start too many projects — don't finish
2. Easily discouraged
3. Passive, would rather avoid conflict
4. Easily distracted
5. Untrusting

Second, determine whether the lists are accurate. Useful here are the various sources of information we discussed in chapter 2. They give us perspective. And so long as we do not surrender our own agency in the process, a *trusted* friend can help. Here is an edited response by a trusted friend (1) of the woman and (2) of the man whose evaluations appear above.

About the woman:
1. Pessimistic about everything.
2. Willing to share food, time, watch kids, do anything to help; *very* much full of charity.
3. Friendly, but seem to have a protective wall around you to prevent close relationships; but we ignore it and enjoy your friendship.
4. Very closed person. Hard to get to know, but once we got past that shield we found a loving, caring person.
5. We feel your friendship and enjoy you. You're very compassionate.

About the man:
1. Always searching for friendship.
2. Cut people sometimes to the point of hurting them without realizing it.
3. Show a great amount of love for fellowmen. Hug, shake hands, give of self and time, material possessions. Would give someone the shirt off your back.
4. Appear to sit around and be waited on by wife and children.
5. Give time to everyone but family. Church, politics, Boy Scouts, school.

Throughout this exercise it is important to keep your strengths well in mind. This is not an exercise in self-punishment.

Write the strengths and weaknesses lists rapidly. It is important to jot down the strengths and weaknesses as they occur to you. Too much deliberation will distort the spontaneity of your reactions. The question is what you feel *right now* are strengths and weaknesses. There is time later for thoughtful revision.

Third, having made the lists, jot down by each item the consequences if the characteristic continues. Good traits need to continue and be refined. Bad traits need to be eliminated.

Fourth, assign priorities to the items on the list. Your values will influence your selections. Remember that this is the beginning of a lifelong project. You are simply learning how to begin the work, so select one or two traits that can be dealt with within a month or less. As self-discipline itself becomes a habit, you can deal with longer-range traits.

Fifth and last, act now on your decisions. Measure your progress daily. Don't rationalize progression or regression. Enjoy and mark your successes. Admit your failures but don't dwell on them.

That is all. It is simple, though at times it may not be easy. It is a process of winning small but important victories. Such victories ought not to go unappreciated.

Experience shows that these lists can be very successful in developing self-discipline. Greg, a tall, slender young man, eighteen years of age, for the first time in several interviews spoke firmly, confidently: "I am gaining control of myself; I lift weights, and I run every day. The weights are increasing and the distance I can go gets longer and longer. It makes me feel very good about myself!" His smile bespoke a brighter opinion of himself than ever before, and it was rare that this rather troubled fellow thought well of himself. His history was replete with painful, failed relationships. His heart was nearly deadened to emotional matters. Yet through working and achieving a deliberate goal he was beginning to think well of himself.

One woman listed "being too talkative" as a weakness. The friend with whom she shared the list (or in this case just the trait, for this woman, as with many other people, never felt like sharing the whole list) challenged her by pointing out that her husband was very quiet by nature, not just because of his wife's verbosity. When she asked her husband about it he told her he was glad she did the talking, because he did not feel comfortable talking to strangers or casual acquaintances. What annoyed him was pressure from her for him to be talkative. By this understanding they enriched what was already a strong relationship.

Leon listed as a weakness "changing my mind too often." His most trusted friend was his wife, so he discussed this trait with her. She suggested that his wish to be responsive to others' needs accounted for some of his apparent changes of mind. Leon weighed his perceptions and his wife's and concluded that he would do well to be more consistent while still carefully considering others. He realized that too much well-meaning inconsistency actually upset those he was concerned about.

The contents of lists such as we are discussing vary as widely as the personalities and characters of those who compose them. There are certain absolutes such as courtesy, marital fidelity, honesty, and personal cleanliness. But most of the items on these lists need to be viewed with as much individual perspective as possible. Erik Erikson spoke to this. "You don't just prove or disprove [such traits], but learn to observe the changes and then decide whether the terms you first chose to name the strengths and weaknesses are the right words" (Elizabeth Hall, "A Conversation with Erik Erikson," *Psychology Today*, June 1983, p. 27).

Nancy was struggling for mental, spiritual, and financial survival following a divorce. Realizing that her children needed a better future than their past had been she took stock of her strengths and weaknesses. She listed as a strength her ability to improvise solutions to almost any challenge. At the same time she listed as a weakness her pessimism about ever coping with the mountainous problems she faced as a single parent. She invited a trusted friend to join with her in evaluating these traits. Together they established a perspective that helped Nancy cope very effectively. She concluded that beyond a certain point her very creative, even ingenious, improvisations became disorganized, inefficient flailings leading nowhere in particular. To a degree her "pessimism" actually was mature recognition of the consequences of being left with several children and few resources.

Nancy began to organize her thinking to focus her considerable creative capacity. She gradually replaced pessimism with clear-headed appraisal of challenges. She increasingly enjoyed an invigorating sense of progress as, one by one, her problems were solved.

Nancy's experience demonstrated what must follow the making of "virtue and vice" lists. Negative traits and habits must be destroyed, positive ones refined. This is not the same procedure as replacing bad with good. Rather, it is a clear-cut task of targeting a trait as detrimental and then eradicating it; similarly, of identifying a trait as benevolent and then refining or expanding it. It feels very good when someone works to achieve a goal he has deliberately set. On the other hand, achievements that occur by chance or are dependent on others' favors can actually undermine self-discipline.

Forging Good Habit Chains

Visualize a behavior chain. Its links are made of actions and moods and circumstances. It is a living chain that pulsates with en-

ergy and can expand or contract. Links are added or removed as
willed by the person who controls it. This chain connects the heart
with the mind and leads to a habitual behavior response. So long
as each link is in place, strong impulses will be transmitted over the
living links of the chain and will guarantee the habitual act. The
surest way to prevent a bad act is to sever some links. Good acts
always follow positive links. Because this is a living chain, bad
links can grow back, so the more links that are severed the greater
the barriers to regrowth. Good links can replace the bad.

In seeking to improve her behavior chain, Nancy went through
the long list of financial and legal tasks she faced. She set priorities.
Then she gathered pertinent information from people and documents. Her math skills were inadequate to do even basic budget-
ing, but after several tries over several weeks she learned the necessary skills. At first all she accomplished was to keep track of how
frequently and how far she strayed from the household budget — a
straying that took place because she would attempt to improvise
rather than follow the plan. Eventually there came a time when she
followed the plan long enough to know by arithmetic that she had
eliminated her impulsiveness.

These improved habits felt good to her mind and heart. One
consequence was that she became less contentious in relations with
others, partly because of reduced financial worry and a sense of
personal growth. She was forging a golden chain of self-discipline
to replace the leaden one that had weighed so heavily on her.
Eventually she defined herself as a capable problem-solver instead
of a "loser."

Skilled musicianship requires the accumulation of basic
thoughts and actions that are practiced — refined — until they ha-
bitually produce the intended music. Isn't it logical that the same
process would apply to skills in human relationships? An example
both of habitual musical skill and human decency was recorded by
the superb violinist, Yehudi Menuhin:

> A month or so before I was to start a South American tour which
> included a recital in Guatemala City, a letter reached me in San
> Francisco from Guatemala City's resident conductor, a man called
> Paco. Its substance was: "Forgive us if we seem presumptuous.
> Knowing you were coming here, we wondered if you would con-
> sider performing the Beethoven Concerto with us. We shall per-
> fectly understand if you refuse. We are not very good but we will

work before you come, and if, at rehearsal, you find us impossible, you must say so honestly; it will already have been a privilege to go through it with you. . . ."

Such a request could not be denied. I suggested that if the rehearsal went well, we would perform together in the second half of my scheduled concert. When I arrived I was touched beyond words. Not only had Paco rehearsed the orchestra every day for a month; he had rehearsed every section and every individual player. Each detail was in place, each note in rhythm and in tune, each *piano* and each *forte* observed. Yes, there have been greater performances, but here was utter conscientious integrity and Beethoven shone through it all undiminished. (Yehudi Menuhin, *Unfinished Journey* [New York: Alfred A. Knopf, 1977], p. 312.)

As simple thoughts and actions become second nature, a person is better prepared to deal with complex relationships. Janet's experience shows this. Janet had a habitual chain of self-disapproval, with alternating links of hard work and impulsive indulgence. A consequence was that she feared she was a failure, unable to discipline herself to do anything well. She made extraordinary efforts to do certain things, did some things very well, yet had failed in two marriages.

For years she had viewed herself as weak, immoral, dependent on others — especially men — and not too bright. To destroy the habits associated with these weaknesses she began by refining her strengths. One strength was writing. She didn't write novels; she wrote to improve her grammar enough to type for income. As a result her typing skills became strong. Her spelling, punctuation, and general sense of construction improved. In a matter of weeks Janet was able to take on typing jobs at home that brought in sorely needed supplemental income.

From these beginnings this woman continued to refine herself through increasing levels of skill. After a few years she had so many good habits that she actually began to believe that she could do what she set her mind to as long as the goal was reasonable. And in fact she did. She never lost sight, though, of how lonely and despairing someone can be when she is convinced she has little to offer. From Janet's own growth evolved an empathy for and an ability to nurture others.

Ten years after she began to make the turnaround she sent a note that said, among other things: "I am working [at a new job] as a clerk typist. My typing skills are 90 correct words per minute. Thank you, my friend . . . for believing in me and my worth and abilities." The friend recalled times when, in anger, Janet had denied any worth or ability, with almost the same anguish as that in which Aldonza had cried out to Don Quixote. (See chapter 3.)

Leisure and Work

Work is part of self-discipline. Apart from speech, how people use their bodies and minds is the most obvious indicator of self-discipline or lack of it. It is probable that leisure use and work use substantially define any woman or any man. I do not recall one person whom I have counseled or observed closely who truly enriched or healed important relationships without a balanced development of strong habits of work and play.

God's words to Adam and Eve seem paradoxical unless we recognize the value of work: "Cursed is the ground for thy sake . . . in the sweat of thy face shalt thou eat bread" (Genesis 3:17, 19). Both sacred and profane history offer clear examples of the consequences of society's attitudes about work.

Millions of struggling believers see Jesus of Nazareth as an ally in life's tribulations because he was a working man, a carpenter. He himself characterized his ministry as that of a shepherd, one who walked long, dusty distances to tend to the needs of his thirsting and hungering flock.

We can also ask whether there is even a remote chance that a frivolous or undisciplined leisure-seeking man could have coped with the experiences in Gethsemane. "He was withdrawn from them . . . and kneeled down, and prayed, saying, Father, if thou be willing, remove this cup from me: nevertheless not my will, but thine, be done. . . . And being in an agony he prayed more earnestly: and his sweat was as it were great drops of blood falling down to the ground." (Luke 22:41–42, 44.)

Thereafter, as he suffered all that man could do to him, his resolve never broke. Such discipline comes from work habits, not from wishful thinking.

But we must also ask whether self-discipline is shown by unrelenting drudgery. To the contrary! It is shown by an ability to engage in and enjoy refreshing recreation and diversion. Jesus offers a pattern for this too. After speaking to, feeding, and blessing the five thousand, apparently exhausted from all that he had done he "constrained his disciples to get into a ship, and to go before him . . . while he sent the multitudes away. And when he had sent the multitudes away, he went up into a mountain apart to pray: and when the evening was come, he was there alone." (Matthew 14:22–23.)

Refusal or psychological inability to engage in exercise and recreation indicates lack of self-discipline, fear of failing, insecurity. The scriptures teach clearly of moderate, refreshing exercise and recreation — Jesus at the wedding feast in Cana, at Mary and Martha's house for a relaxed evening with friends, alone on a mountain to meditate and pray. Similarly the Mormon pioneers found recreation necessary to help them cope with the rigors of their odyssey.

Overcoming the World: The Christian's Task

Those who believe in the gospel of Jesus Christ need to know what God or his prophets have said, for he has always required covenant-based self-discipline from his people. "That is why in the Old Testament when Israel is unfaithful the prophets talk of the nation going a-whoring after strange gods. Israel and God are married and infidelity is like adultery." (William Barclay, *Ethics in a Permissive Society* [London: Harper and Row, 1971], p. 15.) This jealous God requires fidelity from his bride, Israel, because if she is unfaithful she will deprive herself of all that the bridegroom wishes to bestow upon her. It is not enough that men and women be good in the lukewarm sense of being inoffensive and refraining from mischief. There are these good people everywhere. Israel's God offers eternal life with him in a glorious home as the grand reward for those who here choose to discipline themselves enough to conform their behavior and their relationships to his covenants. That means forsaking the world in favor of obedience to God's commandments.

This same God was sent to earth by his Father to complete the redeeming work. His teachings at the Last Supper were recorded by the beloved Apostle, John, in which Jesus announced, "Be of good cheer; I have overcome the world" (John 16:33). Thus, certain of his control of himself during the trials ahead, he completed his work. Later he appeared to the same Apostle in the great revelation on Patmos. His words to John now, with the Crucifixion and the Resurrection behind him, are eternally significant and speak of exalted relationships: "Behold, I stand at the door, and knock: if any man hear my voice, and open the door, I will come in to him, and will sup with him, and he with me. To him that overcometh will I grant to sit with me in my throne, even as I also overcame, and am set down with my Father in his throne." (Revelation 3:20–21.)

Summary

Self-discipline is an effort required of anyone who wishes to enrich or to heal his relationships. It is part of civilized maturity. It is also part of a covenant relationship with God. It is acquired step by step as it is practiced and refined into a living chain. It is inconceivable that a follower of Christ would consider himself capable of enriching or healing relationships while lacking the ability to discipline behavior with himself and with other people.

There are many methods by which to achieve self-discipline. Many books and articles are available that specify techniques, but all are based upon the same principle: work, mental and emotional. It is as Shakespeare's Hamlet says to Queen Gertrude:

> O, throw away the worser part of it,
> And live the purer with the other half.
> . . . .
> Assume a virtue, if you have it not.
>   . . . . Refrain to-night;
> And that shall lend a kind of easiness
> To the next abstinence; the next more easy;
> For use almost can change the stamp of nature,
> And either curb the devil, or throw him out
> With wondrous potency. (Act 3, scene 4.)

Achievement of at least basic self-discipline opens the door to the next phase, self-understanding. Without self-understanding a person is only partially defined, and his or her relationships can be uncertain and unstable.

Self-Understanding

CHAPTER EIGHT

In this chapter and the succeeding three we address the subject of
self-understanding in an eternal context. This part of enriching or
healing relationships comes last because it is not readily accomplished unless it follows earnest efforts to define and discipline
oneself. However, to maintain the enrichments or healings of the
first two, self-understanding is necessary. Paradoxical as it may
seem, although self-definition and self-discipline must come first,
they are in fact ways to get at self-understanding.

Ignorance of self can have severe consequences for our relationships. How can we understand others, or they us, if we are
strangers to ourselves?

Many of us learn to ignore ourselves. Day in and day out in
front of the bathroom mirror we brush our teeth or comb our hair
without "seeing" the person to whom we are doing these things.
Oh, we may take note of the face. We wish we had smaller ears,
straighter teeth. But do we know and understand and respect the
person inside that body?

One of life's purest pleasures is to watch the infant who is discovering his body. He holds his hands out and scrutinizes them. Then, through some mysterious process, eventually understands that they are parts of his identity.

Throughout life we act, then we understand; we act further, then we understand more. As relationships develop, we act, then we understand; then we act further and understand more. In this book up to now, in considering ways to enrich or heal relationships we have been taking the actions and doing the work of self-definition and self-discipline. Now it is timely to understand ourselves and our relationships.

A young father wrote about a discovery that affected his relationships.

> We had a new pup in our home. One day as he was venturing around the house, he came face to face with an identical pup. Needless to say, he'd found the full-length mirror in the bedroom. As he growled and whined I went to see what the problem was. For all my efforts I couldn't convince or satisfy him he was seeing himself. As I laughed, a very cold reality hit me. How often do we find faults that scare and irritate us in others? How sad the Lord must feel with his arm around us trying to open our eyes to our own reflection, not to degrade or humiliate us but so that we can recognize and deal with the reflection.

A young woman struggled hard to cope with relationships. She was uneasy with many people. Despite these anxieties she went to a foreign and primitive country to serve the poorest people. Through this work she began the process of self-understanding. She wrote: "I've never known this kind of peace and happiness. And I know this is a vital step for the beginning of the rest of my life."

Self-understanding is not some trendy, superficial game. It is a plumbing of the depths of who we are. Understanding himself frees a person from unfounded fears, dislikes, and distorted expectations that invariably harm relationships. As we begin to know ourselves we can refine what needs refining, change or adapt, and learn what to expect from ourselves. As we accept ourselves, too, we cease to crave others' opinions of who we are and who we ought to be.

A woman constantly struggled to express herself verbally. Her intelligence, attractive appearance, and quick wit when among close friends belied the inhibitions she strongly felt when among strangers. These inhibitions had caused her to hurry through several experiences, such as high school, without pausing to enjoy friendships or extra-curricular activities. She developed a fine ability to write. Eventually she came to a breakthrough understanding of herself that she wrote about in poetic form.

> Vocally I was not adequate.
> Attention I shunned.
> Fear was a longtime acquaintance.
> I found another way to communicate.
>
> I begin to write.
> My feelings splash out through the pen.
> Words continue to flow.
> My mind races with ideas.
>
> What are the meanings of these words?
> A person and her views
> Expressed in writing, yet so real,
> So many attempts to reach the world.
>
> My family I value with no limits.
> Memories leave my mind to relocate on paper.
> Picturing each face causes me to smile.
> Some scenes hurt my heart.
> Time has gone yet comes again
> With the break of each new day.
> Only photos and words know the past.
>
> Books live for eternity,
> Secrets pass on with each reader;
> Rules of happiness.
> To write a work of such value,
> Each truth comes from reality.
> I will write of reality.

Self-understanding can permit us to break loose from the omnipresent tyrant "They." "They" expect this of us. "They" are not pleased with us. "They" will fire us. "They" will embarrass us.

"They" will reject us, hurt us. "They" are parents, teachers, childhood playmates, people at work, church officers —anyone who explicitly or subtly influences our definition of ourselves. As long as "they" bear heavily down upon us, we are unsure and anxious. Even if "they" praise us highly, we remain subject to "their" opinions and judgments. We relate to others and ourselves by what "they" have expected of us over the years.

"There was a famous Jewish rabbi called Zusya. Sometimes he used to wish that he was other than he was. And then he said very wisely: 'In the world to come they will not ask me, why were you not Moses? They will ask, why were you not Zusya?' " (William Barclay, *Ethics in a Permissive Society* [London: Harper and Row, 1971], p. 95.)

People who come to understand who they are do so by taking, among others, the steps of (1) understanding their family relationships and (2) understanding their personality and their character.

*Children, obey your parents
in the Lord: for this is right.
Honour thy father and
mother. . . . And, ye fathers,
provoke not your children to
wrath: but bring them up in
the nurture and admonition
of the Lord.
— Ephesians 6:1, 2, 4*

Self-Understanding: Family Relationships

CHAPTER NINE

T he most powerful relationships and the most lasting are those between parent and child. Good ones usually but not always mean that a person accepts himself as being of worth. Bad ones may instill a sense of inadequacy, even shame. And pain from certain unhappy family relationships never goes away with just the passage of time. Conversely, happy family relationships in one's youth are enduring in their impact. I know two fine people from different families who were enriched by the same priceless gift from their parents. The man was told nearly every day during his growing-up years that he was loved and cherished. The woman was treated by her mother as a blessing from heaven. Now years later, each of these people is armored against crippling assaults from life's disappointments, for they live each day with the security of knowing that they are loved.

If you are building or enriching a relationship it is important to understand the quality of family love by which your character was formed. When that quality was reassuring love, two responses are now in order: (1) daily pray in gratitude for such a gift; and (2), be compassionate to anyone who was not given such a gift.

Most people can blame their parents for some failure in raising them. Some can even charge their parents with wicked abuse. But in dealing with relationship problems that stem from inadequate or even cruel upbringing by parents what will change by assigning blame? Does the heart ache less if one despises the person who inflicted the wound? Is the mind clearer for hating the people who were inconsistent or even unkind during formative years? If assigning blame relieved distress, revenge would be a preferred tool of emotional healing. But as has been demonstrated since time began, blame, recrimination, and revenge are corrosive emotions and behaviors, not healing ones. A person who adopts hate as a value endangers his own self-esteem, among other personal qualities.

Understanding family relationships becomes, then, a means of appreciation or reconciliation, not of judgment; a matter of gathering facts, not of issuing indictments. Some of these facts are richly laden with pleasant memories. Some may carry with them dark, morbid recollections. But the challenge nevertheless is to seek *facts* and not be diverted by emotions or unfounded opinions.

Thus it is that we can often draw strength from the realities of past relationships. One young woman recalled the safety of her father's strength, and of his attention to her throughout her childhood and teen years; and by this memory she measured the behavior of the young men she dated. Another woman, this one with mixed recollections, resented her father's insistence in her youth that she fight her own battles with others; but in later years, as she put things in perspective, she concluded that while he could have been more emotionally demonstrative, on the whole he had tried to help her become strong enough to prepare for the demands of adulthood.

To begin self-understanding through knowing more about family relationships, then, we must gather facts. A first step is to make a listing of significant relationships with certain people and the situations in which they had impact on us.

We all have vivid as well as repressed recollections of people who affected us. They wounded us or they soothed us. They taught us for good or ill. They gave or they took. They ignored or dominated or nurtured us. Our listing must include and describe not only these people and their impact but also those who *ought* to have had impact. Obviously, parents would be on the list; probably grandparents; not every school teacher, but one or two who did have particular influence; certain friends, neighbors, extended relatives; someone who was significantly pleasant or unpleasant; and so forth. Not every contact was eventful, certainly, but a few left lasting impressions. The absence of certain people from the list will itself be an important fact in self-understanding.

The above information can be written or taped or just kept in your mind, depending on the intensity and seriousness of the relationship problems. With the framework in place, you can then fill in details that will help you understand yourself more accurately.

The techniques and sources for filling in details are varied and include memory, oral history, and documents.

Memory and Oral History

Memory is the least reliable source of data, but it can be an excellent investigative prod. It usually needs to be verified by other evidence. Among the more effective memory triggers are family home evenings, holidays, birthdays, family outings, and other special family occasions. It helps if one can bring to recollection both quantity and quality. Were those past special experiences enjoyable or were they disappointing, even miserable? So many people with troubled relationships recall sad Christmases, ignored birthdays, and few if any family outings. The children of alcoholics often recall childhoods wherein their hopes for special days were dashed by parental inebriation. The human mind does not readily recall humdrum events or routines. It seems to cling to the extraordinary occasions that punctuate everyday existence. Absence or distortion of such occasions in the recollection process may give important clues about oneself.

Clinton recalled his mother as supportive and kind, his father as harsh and remote. At about age thirty-four Clinton began withdrawing from relationships with his wife and children. He had a sense of inadequacy and felt this was largely due to his father's unkindness and lack of interest in him. And until his memories of certain experiences could be checked out, his conclusions seemed justified.

But taped oral interviews with a close cousin and an aunt revealed that Clinton's memories were somewhat incorrect. In the day of the tape recorder any one of us can become a fairly effective amateur family historian. Few people can resist talking on subjects about which they hold strong opinions or know something, and any tape recorder with a *good* microphone placed unobtrusively near the speaker will pick up the voices of people talking about family history.

Clinton's mother had now been dead for several years. His father agreed to be interviewed as a way to gather family history. Clinton's relations with his father were uneasy, but, spurred by a seriously deteriorating relationship with his wife, he needed to ask his father questions about painful childhood memories. He felt that direct questions would be too threatening, so he planned several safe ones, such as, "Tell me about the house we lived in?" or, "What was Aunt Jane like?" Other of his father's recollections were triggered by showing family photos and then asking questions.

What were mined over several sessions were lumps of ordinary clay within which were some priceless gems. One of the most valuable of these changed Clinton's belief that his father never showed any pride in him, a belief arising from a persistent recollection of a Sunday when his father shamed him in front of family and friends. Nearing middle age and now a father himself, Clinton still burned with resentment when he recalled the episode. Somewhat offhandedly the father included the story on the tape while unemotionally recounting some other experiences.

The father explained that he and his wife had struck a truce about church and social life. On Sunday afternoons Mother would accompany Father to the park, where he and a few workmates would play horseshoes or softball. In exchange, he would attend church in the morning with her. One Sunday his father planned to take Clinton along to show him off to his workmates. Unfortunately, after church but before the projected park visit, Clinton and some neighbor children chose to hunt frogs, as a result of which the boy muddied his new clothes. On the tape his father wistfully recalled how disappointed he had been at not being able to show off his son to his friends at the park. This account caused

Clinton to begin to revise some of his recollections about child-hood.

In another taping session, one Clinton replayed several times to evaluate, his father referred to some toys he had made for his son. Gifted with his hands, the father made things that he could not afford to buy. He built a bicycle from cast-off parts, a tree hut, a special wagon. For years Clinton had recalled paternal anger around each gift. On tape his father spoke of regret that the boy was so careless that he had broken each one of these things that had been so lovingly crafted. Later, Clinton's cousin and his older sister confirmed the father's versions.

Larry's adjustments resulting from this fact-gathering process were somewhat more complex. He interviewed his mother about some troubling recollections, and her version added to his guilt about being angry at her. His aunt's recollections offered a more balanced picture, however, one that showed Larry trying vainly to please a mother who was seldom satisfied with his efforts. Thus Larry learned about and had to deal with some of his mother's weaknesses. This meant that in revising upward his opinion of himself he had to see his mother more objectively. And what he saw was not pleasant at first. He went through a phase of anger at her, even loathing. Eventually, though, he reached that stage which gives considerable peace. He saw her as a human being. He gathered information about her parents — his grandparents. He learned that his mother had been raised in poverty, in which every day was a battle to survive. He then measured her adult life against her childhood and saw, factually, that she had overcome many obstacles.

Clinton discovered that he had misinterpreted his father's reactions, even though they were harsh. Larry's research enabled him to put his mother in perspective and forgive her, just as he hoped his children someday would forgive him for being less than perfect.

Documents

Report cards, family scrapbooks, journals, letters, and other documents offer valuable insights, whether we wrote them or received them. Photographs, collections of crayon drawings, love letters scribbled by a childish hand — all can give understanding of the love that pervaded childhood. Parents whose relationships bring forth such things bless their children even in adulthood. Sometimes these collections can even give healing perspective.

Leon had a firmly entrenched self-image of being a poor student and a behavior problem all through elementary and high schools. This caused a mix of guilt and insecurity in relationships, for he assumed that people generally saw him as unpleasant and dumb. As a married man in his thirties he found a box containing his old report cards and some of his letters that his mother had kept. To his surprise, the grades were generally Bs, with a few As and Cs. The cards' comments about behavior were that he was restless, inquisitive, but generally well-mannered and pleasant. This placed in perspective a teacher he had admired and who had, so he recalled, grown to dislike him. But his report cards revealed her appreciation of his potential, along with growing concern about his slothful approach to study.

Leon had also written letters in his late teens. In them he had expressed awareness of his weaknesses and a determination to overcome them. As he read the letters in maturity he realized that he had, in fact, overcome several of those weaknesses. It gave him a boost to realize that he had set some goals and met them.

As with the other elements and steps we have been discussing, if this one is disregarded the effort to build or enrich or heal relationships will likely fall short or take longer than needed. To trust others sensitively we must understand ourselves. We must know how we came by the emotions, traits, and values that bear upon our behavior toward other people. Ignorance of these factors is not blissful; it is harmful. For example, someone whose "scrapbook" contains pleasant souvenirs needs to respect the struggles of a spouse who has no souvenirs. A wife who recalls enjoyable family outings needs to fathom the stark reality that her husband has no such recollections. Yet together they can create their own memories.

Here is an excerpt from a nineteenth-century housewife's journal. Her great-granddaughter reading this a hundred years later could and probably would gain insight into her own twentieth-century burdens as contrasted with those of her ancestor of three generations before.

28 March: "Did not attend church . . . unpleasant Easter Day."

20 June: "Went to Baptist church in the evening. Mrs. Knapp ranted."

27 April [weary of housecleaning]: "One by one . . . the mountains diminish into molehills."

28 April: "The worst is over now. [In the kitchen]"

13 Nov: "A day of hard work . . . but I am accustomed to that."

8 Oct: "An invalid today. But if I am sick I only have to work the harder so it does not pay."

18 June: "A home day. The figure-head [husband?] looked on while the slaves [the rest of the family?] labored."

6 Sept: "Aunt Sophia came up and assisted me at the wash-tub. Very romantic life." (Peter Gay, *Education of the Senses*, vol. 1 of *The Bourgeois Experience: Victoria to Freud* [New York: Oxford University Press, 1984], pp. 172–73.)

Diaries and journals are messages from past family members to those of the future. They strike the heart with especial urgency. They speak intimately to us because we are their flesh and blood descendants. We write to our posterity in the hope that they will pay heed to what we have learned, partly in their behalf.

One journalist recorded her thoughts while crossing the Great Plains in 1862. From it we glimpse the daily travail and infer her strength of character as she writes of "the pleasure of sitting in a large rocking chair, the first time in five months." (Thomas Mallon, *A Book of One's Own* [New York: Ticknor and Fields, 1984], p. 49.)

Journals, diaries, and poetry, however rugged, deserve special attention. They are attempts to express privately what is inexpressible publicly. They may be the truest understandings of self. This may be what sets the Gospel of John apart from the others. The beloved Apostle wrote in intimate biographical terms of Jesus' last mortal days as he recorded the Son obeying and serving the Father.

Healing Family Relationships

For some children family relationships were unquestionably harmful. These the grown-up has to get into factual perspective, or he will be corroded by bitter resentment. However, perspective does not mean avoiding or repressing the facts. What follow are several stories of troubled family relationships. In each one you can simply replace the damaging incidents with positive ones to get a vivid picture of how to enrich relationships or heal troubled ones.

Lorna's father had sexually abused her from age five until, at age thirteen, she could keep him at bay. Her anguish was like that of most victims of incest: she doubted herself; she wondered why her mother had not protected her; she alternated between needing a father and hating the man who should have been her protector but in fact was her enemy. Later in counseling, over a four-year period Lorna struggled with these powerful emotions. Finally she replaced the subjective labels of *father* and *enemy* with facts about the human being: he was a pathetic, weak, utterly self-focused person who was, in fact, her biologic father but, in fact, her emotional attacker. Now she pitied him. By this breakthrough she began also to place other people and circumstances in perspective.

One of the most revealing experiences of my career took place when I was with Lorna as she confronted her father several years later. By then he had remarried. It was necessary for Lorna to obtain his signature on a legal paper. There, with his new wife in the room, Lorna calmly asked him why he had sexually abused her. He refused to answer. He gave no indication that he even heard the question. For nearly one hour or so this man registered no apparent reaction. It was as if he had turned an inner dial and switched channels. He spoke about the legal paper. He mentioned his new wife and his hobbies. He was lucid. But of his crimes he said nothing, showed nothing.

For me, a virtually silent spectator, the text books came alive. I saw firsthand how such a person really did lack the emotions universally expected of parents. I also saw a child, now an adult, maturely and calmly require an explanation from the man who, in her childhood, had terrified her, whose violations had left her angry and confused for so long.

Like other children who have confronted but not attacked parents with whom they have had traumatic relationships, Lorna gained a victory. She did not condemn her father. Instead, she saw him as he was. She also gained an appreciation of her mother and what she had endured for many years.

In other cases parent-child discussions of the past can bear healing fruit. A therapy group was designed for sexually troubled families. They began by the adults listing family values about sex, authority, money, what makes people attractive — a variation of our significant relationships list. Then the adolescents were asked to make a similar list. Finally the children were asked to tell what they had heard their parents and older siblings say about these issues.

"The halting presentation of the younger children provided a painful perspective for everyone [and] brought glistening tears to parents' eyes. The overwhelming expression of sadness and loneliness was incredibly poignant as the adults recognized that what their own children were experiencing now was but an echo of their own early years." (Patrick Carnes, *The Sexual Addiction* [Minneapolis: Comp Care Publications, 1983], p. 132.)

Whatever the immediate outcome, most people whose relationships are crippled must confront their family's past. By doing so they deal with manageable facts rather than with unmanageable fear. And they do not linger in the past. They put it in perspective so that they can deal with the here and now as well as with the future.

Confronting the past is possible even when one's parents and other significant relatives are dead. Letters can be written that express long-suppressed feelings. It is not uncommon for people to visit the graves of relatives and talk as if they could hear. Relief comes not from morbid fascination with the symbols of death but with expressing pent-up emotions: often these are a mixture of anger and love. Prayer can be especially healing as the supplicant asks for divine help to convey forgiveness and love to those who left unhealed wounds behind them.

Erma Bombeck related an important memory, but without her usual humor. She nostalgically recalled her father, his kindness and dependability, particularly his regular going to work and returning. Then: "One morning my father didn't get up and go to work. He went to the hospital and died the next day. I didn't know his leaving would hurt so much." (*Family: The Ties That Bind . . . and Gag!* [New York: McGraw-Hill, 1987], p. 2.)

Leanne hurt for different reasons. She hurt as she recalled her absent father. She had not seen him in the ten years since her parents divorced. She saw or talked with her authoritarian mother weekly, and then hurt even more. Despite a college education, success in a challenging profession, effective leadership in various church positions, Leanne feared intimate relationships. Her own marriage was breaking up. She did not understand herself.

An incident I was involved in was revealing. I phoned her to change an appointment, with the intent to relieve some scheduling pressure on Leanne because that week she had many other commitments. In contrast to our usual courteous though guarded exchanges, this time Leanne was abrupt, even sharp. The next time we met I asked what had offended her. She was surprised, not recalling any such reaction. She had been relieved to reschedule the appointment. Then Leanne made an important self-discovery. She said: "I didn't know how to react to such a thoughtful gesture. I really don't know how to be comfortable with people in authority." From this point she better understood significant family relationships that still influenced her.

After ten years of marriage, Carolyn feared she was losing her children and her husband. She was constantly angry with them, resenting their demands on her. Tumbling about in the rush of daily living, she just reacted until things were so emotionally fouled up that she sought professional help. A key to regaining control of her life was that she pause long enough to understand herself against her family background.

As if regurgitating poison, Carolyn wrote about some recollections. First she noted that she came from a prominent family, her father being very well known in the community and the church. Here are excerpts from her letter, in which she reported the profound though painful self-understanding that opened up the way to healing:

> My parents had and still have one of the emptiest, [most] loveless, and hostile marriages that could possibly be called a marriage. It was not a marriage in any real sense of the word. I grew up in a home with tremendous undercurrents of anger, hostility, unhappiness, and bitterness. I was used by my mother as a sounding board for all her complaints about my father because his autocratic control did not allow her to communicate with him in any real way. His style was to retreat behind a newspaper every night, and go into days-long pouts when he was mad at her. His church work was a very convenient escape from the home, year after year. I never saw my parents embrace except a perfunctory kiss as he left the house each morning. I never saw them kiss in an affec-

tionate way, and I never saw their arms around each other in affection. Likewise, my father never hugged me, and never told me he loved me until I was at least thirty-five years old. I could go on and on—no affection, extreme criticism, no real talking, but all of the surface appearances of a model family. Each of us children acquired their own style of compensation (mine was "super-achiever"), but for me the underlying result was a deep hostility toward men and particularly for any kind of "unrighteous dominion." I could not at any level make sense of the upward climb of my father in the church and community with the failure in the home.

You must realize that at best, as a teenager, most of these feelings were unconceptualized and unrealized. They were there so deep, but it took many years to understand what had occurred. My spirit deeply rebelled at autocratic control and the "doormat" posture of my mother, but unfortunately for me and the man I married, I didn't understand what was really going on within me.

I went ahead and married a man who could not (because of his background) be anything else but a perpetuation of what I deeply resented. I had always been known as an aggressive person, and many people saw my husband as the weaker part of the partnership, but his dominance and control came in many ways in the home that others did not see, and some I was not even consciously aware of.

I went into the marriage with these deep hostilities, and we reaped the rewards immediately. Because of the lack of trust and the hostility (on both our parts) there was no real intimacy. My husband and I triggered each other's pain all the time and constantly failed to fulfill each other's expectations because we were so dependent. (He came from a totally autocratic home also, with a mother who took out her frustrations by being over-controlling with her children.) We were failing badly in our marriage—[but] we kept up all the appearances of another generation of model family.

Our sexual relationship was very stressful at times. I rarely wanted to make love. When we engaged in sex, it was very empty. I almost always experienced orgasm, but there was never a real feeling of closeness and glow afterwards, and very little touching and affection before. I felt constantly cheated, but had no idea what was really going on within myself. I know now that, literally, something in my makeup made it impossible for me to experience sex in the full physical and emotional sense. I was in an emotional and physical straightjacket, and I literally did not "feel" in the precise meaning of that word.

Four years ago, I was devastated by the discovery that for half of our ten years of marriage, my husband had been sexually involved with several different women. The buried rage and hostility that had been building for so many years just totally exploded within me. I experienced the deepest hate and bitterness that you can imagine. It just about destroyed me.

Carolyn's crisis forced her to look for reasons for her defective relationships. As devastating as was her indictment of her parents, she found no relief in blaming them. She was angry, as her letter states, but the first steps toward peace of mind were to understand herself. She had to stop being a child hurt by the vast divergence between her parents' public image and their private lives. She had to be a grown-up and see her parents as human beings who may have been intentional hypocrites or just may have been two people trying to overcome their own unhappy backgrounds.

True, had Carolyn's parents been faithful to the teachings of Christ she would not have been so afflicted or vulnerable. From their weaknesses we can extrapolate what are essential virtues in family life: affection, respect, enjoyable activities, integrity of behavior and values, Christlike speech and actions. Indeed, section 4 of the Doctrine and Covenants lists such traits: faith, charity, virtue, knowledge, temperance, patience, kindness, humility, love, with an eye single to the glory of God.

So we must ever remember that certain basic Christlike traits enrich family relationships. Violation of them wounds. What was very pertinent was that Carolyn had married a man who fit the old pattern, and together they constructed a family style quite similar to or worse than that of either of their parents. With this self-understanding, Carolyn was able to trace those thoughts and habits that interfered with her present situation. As she began to understand herself she began to define herself. By the time she wrote the above letter her wounds were healing.

Erica, a strong, decent woman in her late forties, had struggled with an enslaving habit since she was thirteen. Willpower and counseling had not freed her, for she had little self-understanding. One evening, as she discussed her "captor" with a church leader, she came to understand that due to certain family experiences her bad habit was actually her tried and true way of feeling cared for, even when others were unkind to her. Immediately upon understanding her real motivation, she was freed of a great weight.

Some time later she wrote about the self-understanding she had experienced and how it led to healing relationships.

> I have never experienced such a tremendous breakthrough in such a short period of time. Were you able to see the doors that were opening for me? All the lights that were coming on? It was all happening so fast I could hardly keep up with it. It was as though a wall inside me broke and love came pouring out. I wanted to go home and call my grown children and tell them that I loved them. Which I did, and they were surprised. It feels like that little piece of knowledge was the last piece in the puzzle to knowing all of myself. . . . I realize I will still have to work to overcome old habits so that I will not regress, but it is a wonderful feeling to have this knowledge.

A valuable document, for family purposes as for others, is the Bible. The fifth commandment is ripe with meaning about self-understanding. "Honour thy father and thy mother: that thy days may be long upon the land which the Lord thy God giveth thee" (Exodus 20:12).

The lengthier version in Deuteronomy 5:16 increases our understanding: "Honour thy father and thy mother, as the Lord thy God hath commanded thee; that thy days may be prolonged, and that it may go well with thee, in the land which the Lord thy God giveth thee."

Mark's Gospel records Jesus as clarifying it even further: "For Moses said, Honour thy father and thy mother; and whoso curseth father or mother, let him die the death of the transgressor, as it is written in your law" (JST, Mark 7:12).

Here we see an impressive values consistency bridging the Hebraic and the Christian eras, one which meets the test that scientists call reliability. Children are commanded to honor their parents; not worship, but honor them. Why? Because human relationships are more complete when the generations are linked together. People so bound together have a sense of place in history. (See Erik Erikson, *Childhood and Society* [New York: W. W. Norton and Company, 1963], p. 268.)

This is so crucial to· relationships that Jehovah promised his people that he would send Elijah the prophet to "turn the heart of the fathers to the children, and the heart of the children to their fathers, lest I come and smite the earth with a curse" (Malachi 4:6). This sending of Elijah was accomplished about 2300 years later (see D&C 110:13–16). Today on all sides incontrovertible evidence accumulates of the destruction wrought by failure to honor family bonds and covenants. Can any other conclusion be drawn than that a curse has fallen upon the family of man and that, as in the case of the plagues upon Pharaoh, no remedy is to be found other than obedience to God's laws?

Summary

Delving into your family background is not an exhaustive research of every past event. Rather, it is an organized way to look at significant episodes in significant relationships. Memory, oral history, and the use of documents aid self-understanding.

A friend of mine navigated his aircraft all over the world, including war-torn Vietnam. He said he did it by plotting his positions by the stars. To look at and measure by all the stars would have been mentally impossible as well as impractical, so he sighted, adjusted to, and steered by a few significant stars. So it is with this aspect of self-understanding. A few significant relationships are sighted, adjusted to, and steered by to enable the traveler to know where he has been and where he is now, so that he can determine how to get where he wants to go. All parents make mistakes, all families are less than ideal, some are even sick. By our sharing here some examples of troubled family relationships it should be even clearer what ought to be done to continue to build or enrich relationships. And when healing is necessary it is important to understand how the wounds were inflicted, for this determines and permits correct restorative measures.

Understanding family relationships is one part of self-understanding. The other part is to understand our relationship with and within ourselves. We shall address that part in the next two chapters as we examine personality and character.

Then the word of the Lord
came unto me saying, Before I
formed thee in the belly I
knew thee; and before thou
camest forth out of the womb
I sanctified thee.
— Jeremiah 1:4–5

Self-Understanding: Personality and Character

CHAPTER TEN

A particular delight of being a grandparent is to observe grandchildren without experiencing the challenges and frustrations of raising them. This often results in indulgence that parents then need to remedy. Freed of parenting burdens, grandparents can see things they missed while trying to raise their own children. They see the inborn, innate personalities of their grandchildren, the traits, tendencies, even gifts that are not explained by what parents can teach.

There is the fifteen-month-old granddaughter who responds to music by shaking her entire body in rhythm. She was also alert and unusually expressive minutes after her birth. Her brother at two months is quiet, suggesting a contemplative personality. Another grandson, now five, has always been innately dignified and earnest, is easily wounded if embarrassed, but is possessed of a quick wit and a boisterous sense of fun when he is with people he knows well. His sister, nearing nine years, just naturally takes care of her brother and baby sister. She also strives hard to study in school. And, when necessary, she stands firmly for her territorial rights. Her year-old baby sister explores endlessly; nothing is too mundane to ignore. She is fascinated by books and will sit for unusually long periods turning pages and studying the pictures. She shares generously with her cousins.

All these traits are startlingly obvious within the first months, even weeks, of these childrens' lives. How can this be? What does it mean to the enhancement of relationships?

Many parents know that each child is born with innate traits that are unique from his brothers and sisters. This is called, in our discussion, *personality*. What the child learns and how he develops from the way he is raised is called *character*. It is a key to self-understanding to know our personality traits — not to rid ourselves of them but to accept and refine them. It is through character growth that we refine our personality traits and become better equipped for relationships. In fact, ignorance of or conflict with our personalities can undermine relationships because it provokes a war within ourselves.

One of the most vivid examples of personality and character is another story about Heber J. Grant. Left financially strapped by the early death of his father, young Heber's determined mother taught him to persevere. This he did with remarkable success. The motto he adopted was "Never despair."

Among the tasks Heber assigned himself later in life was learning to sing in a solo voice. That he lacked innate musical gifts is a major understatement, but through exceptional work he did acquire the ability to carry a tune unaided by other singers. The stark truth, however, is that Heber's singing voice, though sincere, even earnest, and on tune, was not pleasing to the ear of his listeners. Certain of his companions on long trips in horse and buggy have left virtual affidavits that his recitals tended to lengthen, not shorten, the journey.

It says much that Heber was seldom, if ever, *asked* to sing. He tended to declare his intention, and afterwards his almost always captive audiences seemed inclined to agree that he had indeed labored mightily against formidable odds. He himself was aware of this reality. On one long trip Heber undertook to sing a hundred hymns. His companions, taking it as a joke, consented. In Heber's words: "After I had sung about forty tunes, they assured me that if I sang the remaining sixty they would be sure to have nervous prostration. I paid no attention whatever to their appeal, but held them to their bargain and sang the full hundred." (Preston Nibley, *The Presidents of the Church* [Salt Lake City: Deseret Book Company, 1959], pp. 277, 296.)

There really are certain limits to what we can do, and it cannot be counted as moral weakness on our part if we bump up against those limits. Hence, Heber J. Grant had every right to rejoice at his triumph of determination in learning how to carry a tune. But had he judged himself, or been judged by others, as a failure because he never measured up to expectations of quality — or even of pleasing singing — he would have found himself in one of the most debilitating traps of all, that of trying to exceed his inherent limitations. At the same time, he spent his life developing to a high degree character traits such as diligence, honesty, and service. Learning to sing on tune was an acquired, voluntary character trait. Being unable to sing with a richly pleasing voice was an inborn, involuntary, personality trait. Had he been unhappy with his inability to sing with operatic quality, Heber would have considered himself a failure. Instead he set what was an attainable goal, given his very real limitations, but he did not have expectations that would have doomed him to failure. An impossible dream is not a healthy goal. A great and achievable dream is.

Anyone trying to understand himself so that he can enhance or heal relationships needs to ask: "What parts of my behavior are learned and what are inborn?" "What parts of me are character that I can expect to change, and what are personality and cannot be or ought not to be changed?" Those parts that are learned, acquired by experience and the decisions we make — after being born — we are calling *character*.

Coming to a clear understanding of personality and character enables us to enhance relationships by "being ourselves" without frustrating others by our inconsistencies or inner confusion. This promotes deep and lasting healing by calming the inner turmoil that stems from unresolved conflict between who we are and who we are expected to be. Let us examine the matter in some detail.

Debates rage about what is often termed "nature versus nurture." Some scientists claim that biology determines behavior;

others view the human brain as an incomplete computer awaiting programming through learning. At the heart of this controversy lie some of the most significant aspects of understanding ourselves.

Let us consider the biological aspect.

Biology

Scientists are turning up impressive evidence that heredity has a greater influence on one's personality and behavior than either one's upbringing or the most crushing social pressure. The debate over what has been called "nature vs. nurture" seems to be taking a decisive turn.

New results from studies of identical twins—plus a host of findings in behavioral and animal research—are leading many scientists to conclude that genes not only control such physical characteristics as eye color and height but also profoundly influence human behavior and personality. . . . Are we who we are—rich or poor, smart or stupid, outgoing or retiring, aggressive or timid, law-abiding or criminal—because of genetic traits passed down through the ages? . . . Can heredity be overridden through social programs and the way we rear our children? . . .

After exhaustively testing 348 sets of twins, including 44 pairs of identical twins raised separately, [the Minnesota Center for Twin and Adoption Research] concluded that how people think and act—their very personality—is determined more by the DNA in their cells than by society's influences. . . . The research bolsters what parents have always sensed: Even within a single family, each child, right from birth, is different. While parents may have the impression with their first child that they are the prime molders of his or her fate, the arrival of a second baby makes it clear that babies arrive with built-in likes and dislikes. . . .

In this view, the human mind, rather than being a *tabula rasa* to be filled in from birth by family and society, is "hard wired" before birth with a predisposed personality. (John S. Lang, "How Genes Shape Personality," *U.S. News and World Report*, 13 April 1987, pp. 58–66. Copyright, 1987, *U.S. News and World Report*.)

But if biology is the sum total of the matter, then the entire history of human relationships is reduced either to mechanistic exchanges among evolutionary automatons or to a puppet show with humans dancing about on strings manipulated by God.

Richard Restak, a neurologist, voices this in his book, *The Brain*. "Most of us recoil at the idea that our hopes, our dreams, our lusts, and our ambitions may someday be defined in terms familiar only to the neurochemist and the neurophysiologist. Our mind, our free will, our creativity—*surely* these things attest to the presence of something more than the gnarled mass of cells we call the brain."

This same author offers a useful view of the brain-mind versus the soul-spirit.

> Science is concerned with observable, or at least describable, phenomena. . . . To ask, "Is there a soul?," for instance, is not the same thing as asking about the existence of mind. Soul is a religious concept that concerns such things as salvation, eternal life, communication with a deity. . . . Mind, on the other hand, refers to consciousness, memory, and behavior as well as a host of other manifestations of a functioning brain. While many artificial intelligence experts are claiming that certain advanced computers may possess a "mind," no one has ever had the temerity to suggest they possess an immortal soul. Put slightly differently, to deny that a mind exists separately from a brain doesn't imply any position at all on the existence of a soul, God, a hereafter. . . . Neuroscience cannot and should not bolster or undermine these beliefs. There is another reason for maintaining a reasonable degree of humility about readily dismissing the claims of religious thinkers throughout the ages: Our understanding is limited by the organization of our brains. "We now see through a glass darkly," as one mystic [Paul] put it. Certainly it cannot be denied that the organization of our brain places limitations on what we can and cannot know by perception or reason. (Richard Restak, *The Brain* [New York: Bantam Books, 1984], pp. 1, 344.)

What then can we conclude about the impact of biology on relationships? I conclude that there is evidence that we do have some biologic predispositions and that these predispose us to act and react within relationships in certain ways. The energetic personality may be impatient with people who are somewhat passive in nature. The first-grader with an inquisitive personality may annoy a harried teacher whose goal is mass order, not individual initiative. The effervescent personality may enhance an adolescent's ability to survive the rigors of high school relationships. The tender-hearted personality may be severely wounded by abuse or rejection and may turn to destructive relationships.

John Money, a neurology-psychology researcher at the Johns Hopkins University, has studied the effects of hormones and genes on human behavior. He offers useful interpretations of biology's influence. His point is that it may be unrealistic to try to separate biology and psychology too exclusively. Our emotions influence our bodies. Our bodies influence our emotions. What we feel, we express physically. We mentally experience stimuli that we then incorporate into the brain. We physically experience stimuli that we interpret emotionally. We think about nature, and nature forces us to think. Physical beings, we are also emotional and spiritual.

At the conclusion of a closely reasoned, minutely detailed article on male homosexuality, John Money makes this pertinent statement: "It is counterproductive to characterize prenatal determinants of sexual orientation as biological, and postnatal determinants as not. The postnatal determinants that enter the brain through the senses by way of social communication and learning also are biological, for there is a biology of learning and remembering." (See "Sin, Sickness, or Status? Homosexual Gender Identity and Psychoneuroendocrinology," *American Psychologist,* April 1987, pp. 384–99.)

This debate was neatly summed up in a letter to the editor of *Time* magazine in response to an article about nature versus nurture. Social scientists, the letter stated, have "finally acknowledged what most mothers have always known: each child arrives in the world with an individual personality. Psychologists have imposed an enormous burden on parents by insisting that they are somehow solely responsible for their children's personalities. Now parents can sit back and enjoy each child's uniqueness." (*Time,* 19 November 1984, p. 16.)

Freewill and Personal Agency

From another letter to the editor in response to the previously quoted article on genes and personality, I quote this excerpt: "There is a forgotten aspect of a child's development that is totally beyond the influence of the gene factor: Genetics will never play a role in shaping the *values* of a child, which are the key components of his character." (*U.S. News and World Report*, 27 April 1987, p. 6.)

Unfortunately, zealots from both extremes cloud this crucial issue. There is no evidence to support absolute domination of the human mind, let alone the spirit, by biologic programming. But there has always been evidence that a person may not be able to "do anything he makes up his mind to do." The belief in total power of mind over matter has caused mischief and grief.

There are, of course, parts of the human being that are biologic and extremely hard to control voluntarily. Some are obvious and immutable — e.g., breathing.

There are involuntary, biologically caused behaviors that cannot be overridden and that are extremely harmful to relationships. Alzheimer's disease is one. Another can occur if lesions form in the prefrontal lobes of the brain, in which case the victim can lose inhibitions and say things that are inappropriate. Tampering with the brain's lobes led to the rash of prefrontal lobotomies in the 1940s and 1950s. This surgical procedure irreversibly changed excitable, agitated behavior to passivity. It also so dramatically altered personalities that relationships suffered.

Other biologic phenomena are nearly immutable but can be overridden by intense exercise of will or agency. One such is the rare but serious disorder called Gilles de la Tourette syndrome. Its symptoms are tics, repeated nervous mannerisms that are often considered to be psychologic in origin. With Tourette the sufferer has odd, even bizarre, tics that can have devastating physical, emotional, and social consequences. (Perhaps some of these sufferers were burned at the stake in more superstitious times.)

An unfortunate victim may snort until the nose bleeds, snap the head violently, kick, stamp, shriek, and grab genitals — his own or others'. Even more mortifying, the person may impulsively shout out obscenities or epithets. Research suggests that this terrible affliction may have a chemical-neurologic basis, for certain drugs moderate it (but do not cure it). What is so relevant for our present discussion is that some people have exercised sufficient willpower or agency to control these mannerisms.

One victim who became a physician wrote: "I feel like you would if there were a powerful man who had you by the throat and just kept tightening his grip. I end my days exhausted because of the energy I expend both ticquing and warding off the tics." (See Glenn Garelik, "Exorcising a Damnable Disease," *Discover*, December 1986, pp. 74–84.)

One sufferer, Joseph Bliss, kept a diary for thirty-five years detailing his struggle. "There are so many lovely things in the world to experience. . . . And maybe even *yet* some soul-satisfying challenge to meet. But all of this will be dust if every thought and muscle is busy trying to hold back the blinking of an eye." (In Thomas Mallon, *A Book of One's Own* [New York: Ticknor and Fields, 1984], p. 230.)

This extreme condition, when added to all the other examples of willpower any reader can recall, adds up to the fact that much human behavior can be made subject to the mind, the will, personal agency, or character. Even though, as we have stated earlier, mind cannot always overcome matter, we must recognize that there are many instances when it can. To know which is which is one of life's most liberating discoveries, for it justifies our efforts to acquire character traits that enhance or heal relationships.

This was demonstrated in an institution for mentally retarded people. The men and women there ranged from being profoundly limited to those who could feed and dress themselves but were not able to function independently in the outside world. I worked on a ward where few of the residents could speak or care for their private needs. Some were dangerous and needed constant, heavy medication. One had killed an attendant.

I often wondered what emotions stirred within these men and what relationships were important to them, since within the institution their behavior was medically regulated and their relationships institutionalized. Then one Christmas I learned.

It was during a rehearsal for the little program the residents put on for their parents and anyone else who would come. If you have ever been involved with musical efforts of seriously retarded people, you know that perfect pitch is not their forte. I listened as the chorister patiently taught them the words. Getting them to sing on tune was obviously not her priority. I cannot recall which carol it was, but I do recall how I was humbled by the realization that within those limited bodies there functioned whole and powerful spirits.

Each was trying to sing earnestly. One boy tried hardest of all. He wore a football helmet to protect him when he fell during the grand mal epileptic seizures that afflicted him. As he sang, his forehead furrowed in concentration. His face got red. His hands clenched tight. And the cords on his neck stood out. I knew then and I know now that I was witnessing a pure spirit attempt to make an inadequate body obey its yearnings to sing praises to the Redeemer of that body. It also was evidence to me of the reality of the premortal experience. This cannot be called a scientific observation, but it has influenced my professional clinical work ever since.

Even so severe and bizarre an illness as schizophrenia is, so far as is yet known, a combination of inherited personality and learned character. There is evidence of chemical and neurologic factors. There is also evidence of environmental, familial factors. "One also has to remember that the outbreak of any illness is almost always dependent on environmental factors" (Restak, *The Brain*, p. 283). So we must conclude, as always, that we are a complex mixture of inherited and learned traits that add up to personality and character.

Premortal Personality

Does the gospel of Christ give insight into this matter? Most certainly! Judeo-Christian history and modern revelation afford believers a sublime explanation for personality and character, for they teach of our life *prior* to this earthly experience.

In John Milton's *Paradise Lost*, with impressive certitude and his poet's pen the author described heavenly events and the people and relationships that preceded earth life. Others with less charity —especially Calvinists, by their unfortunate belief in predestination—also implied belief in a life prior to this one, for how is one predestined if he did not exist before?

Scripture both ancient and modern contains plenty of references to an earlier existence. Job, that man whose relationship with God was tested to its limits, carried on a conversation with God that assumed premortal experiences and relationships. "Then the Lord answered Job out of the whirlwind, and said. . . . Gird up now thy loins like a man; for I will demand of thee, and answer thou me. Where wast thou when I laid the foundations of the earth? declare, if thou hast understanding. . . . When the morning stars sang together, and all the sons of God shouted for joy?" (Job 38:1, 3-4, 7.)

Jehovah is referred to as "the God of the spirits of all flesh" (Numbers 16:22). It is written that at the death of the body "the spirit shall return unto God who gave it" (Ecclesiastes 12:7; see also Alma 40:11).

Peter referred to the believers in Asia and other places as "elect according to the foreknowledge of God the Father" (1 Peter 1:2). He also wrote that Jesus "was foreordained before the foundation of the world" (1 Peter 1:20).

Paul, the missionary Apostle, wrote to Titus, "In hope of eternal life, which God, that cannot lie, promised before the world began" (Titus 1:2). To whom did God make the promise if not to already existent entities?

Paul testified to the Ephesians: "Blessed be the God and Father of our Lord Jesus Christ, who hath blessed us with all spiritual blessings in heavenly places in Christ: according as he hath chosen us in him before the foundation of the world, that we should be holy and without blame before him in love" (Ephesians 1:3-4).

Paul, who exchanged his Roman-Jewish security for a life of Christian service, also spoke plainly to the Athenians who were steeped in Greek logic and rhetoric: "Whom therefore ye ignorantly worship, him declare I unto you. God that made the world and all things therein, seeing that he is Lord of heaven and earth . . . and hath made of one blood all nations of men for to dwell on all the face of the earth, and hath determined the times before appointed, and the bounds of their habitation; that they should seek the Lord, if haply they might feel after him, and find him, though he be not far from everyone of us: for in him we live, and move, and have our being; as certain also of your own poets have said, for we are also his offspring." (Acts 17:23-28.) It is instructive that Paul, whose education would have allowed him to debate effectively the Greek sophists, here chose simply to testify about God's fatherhood of the preearthly family of spirits.

As quoted earlier, Jeremiah recorded Jehovah's affirmation of their premortal relationship. "Before I formed thee in the belly I

knew thee; and before thou camest forth out of the womb I sanctified thee, and I ordained thee a prophet unto the nations"
(Jeremiah 1:5).

Milton's basis for his epic poem *Paradise Lost* is found in
various places in the Bible:

"And the angels which kept not their first estate, but left their
own habitation, he hath reserved in everlasting chains under darkness unto the judgment of the great day" (Jude 1:6).

"And there was war in heaven: Michael and his angels fought
against the dragon; and the dragon fought and his angels, And
prevailed not; neither was their place found any more in heaven.
And the great dragon was cast out, that old serpent, called the
Devil, and Satan, which deceiveth the whole world: he was cast
out into the earth, and his angels were cast out with him. . . .
Therefore rejoice, ye heavens, and ye that dwell in them. Woe to
the inhabiters of the earth and of the sea! for the devil is come
down unto you, having great wrath, because he knoweth that he
hath but a short time. And when the dragon saw that he was cast
unto the earth, he persecuted the woman which brought forth the
man child." (Revelation 12:7-9, 12-13.)

The brighter part of the premortal experience is recorded in Jehovah's appearance to the brother of Jared. "Behold, I am Jesus
Christ. . . . Seest thou that ye are created after mine own image?
Yea, even all men were created in the beginning after mine own image. Behold, this body, which ye now behold, is the body of my
spirit; and man have I created after the body of my spirit; and even
as I appear unto thee to be in the spirit will I appear unto my
people in the flesh." (Ether 3:14-16.)

A belief in an existence prior to this present life is by no means
uncommon. It was implied in Eileen Cronin-Noe's account of how
she coped with the disastrous circumstances of being a Thalid-
omide baby. She was born without lower legs as a result of this
medication that was given to pregnant women in the late 1950s.

"In kindergarten I asked for the first time, why don't I have
legs?

" 'Because God looked for someone to love extra special. He
chose you to be that person and to carry the cross,' one man explained. But sometimes I suspected that other people thought I
must have done something very wicked in a past life to receive

such a severe punishment!" (*Los Angeles Times,* 22 July 1987, Part V, p. 3.)

Mrs. Cronin-Noe's expression emphasizes how natural it is for the human mind to think of existing with identity in times or places before this mortal life. Such beliefs of course include reincarnation—a previous life in a physical body, a non-Christian concept. For the Christian it is plain that Jesus and his followers discussed premortal behavior and its possible mortal consequences in the context of "a man which was blind from his birth. And his disciples asked him, saying Master, who did sin this man, or his parents, that he was born blind? Jesus answered, Neither hath this man sinned, nor his parents: but that the works of God should be made manifest in him." (John 9:1-3.)

The people of the Qumran community (the Dead Sea Scrolls area), who lived there a century or two before the time of Christ, were taught that prior to this earthly life God at least planned for their existence here. "From the God of knowledge comes all that is and shall be. Before ever they existed he established their whole design, and when, as ordained for them, they come into being, it is in accord with his glorious design that they fulfill their work." (Wayne A. Meeks, *The Moral World: The First Christians* [Philadelphia: The Westminster Press, 1986], p. 77. See also *The Dead Sea Scriptures* in English translation with introduction and notes by Theodor Gaster [Garden City, New York: Anchor Books, 1976], pp. 144-46.)

Summary

There is in both ancient and modern doctrine a sublime explanation of our innate personality traits. Science also offers possibilities for their transmission through biologic inheritance. Recognizing the existence of the personality factor promotes crucial self-understanding as we work to acquire character traits that will enrich our relationships or heal troubled ones.

And all things are of God,
who hath reconciled us to
himself by Jesus Christ, and
hath given to us the ministry
of reconciliation.
—2 Corinthians 5:18

Self-Understanding: Reconciliation of Personality and Character

CHAPTER ELEVEN

F rom reasoned biology and revealed religion and just plain living, there is overwhelming evidence that within us at birth are traits, inclinations, gifts, talents, and tendencies, all of which can be lumped together as *personality*. What we acquire or learn or expand upon after birth is *character*. Conflict between personality and character amounts to civil war within a person. *Reconciling* these two parts is essential to self-understanding. It can help enhance or even heal relationships, for out of this inner reconciliation grows accurate knowledge about what to expect of ourselves and what others may expect of us. In fact the preceding ten chapters of this book are really about the reconciling of personality and character, though they emphasize different aspects. But to stress the importance of reconciliation, we begin this chapter with two examples of how powerful personality and character are and, by implication, how damaging a failure to reconcile them can be. One is from Mark Twain, the other from Dante.

In the description by Samuel Clemens (Mark Twain) of his brother, Orion, we have a vivid representation of personality and character. With his wry clarity, Clemens recorded the impetuous personality and the decent character of his beloved brother and his attempts to reconcile them.

> One of his characteristics was eagerness. He woke with an eagerness about some matter or other every morning; it consumed him all day; it perished in the night and he was on fire with a fresh new interest next morning before he could get his clothes on. He exploited in this way three hundred and sixty-five red-hot new eagernesses every year of his life—until he died sitting at a table with a pen in his hand, in the early morning, jotting down the conflagration for that day and preparing to enjoy the fire and smoke of it until night should extinguish it. He was then seventy-two years old.
>
> But I am forgetting another characteristic, a very pronounced one. That was his deep glooms, his despondencies, his despairs; these had their place in each and every day along with the eagernesses. Thus his day was divided—no, not divided, mottled —from sunrise to midnight with alternating brilliant sunshine and black cloud. Every day he was the most joyous and hopeful man that ever was, I think, and also every day he was the most miserable man that ever was.
>
> During his apprenticeship in St. Louis he joined a number of churches, one after another, and taught in the Sunday schools— changing his Sunday school every time he changed his religion. . . . I may remark here that throughout his long life he was always trading religions and enjoying the change of scenery. I will also remark that his sincerity was never doubted; his truthfulness was never doubted; and in matters of business and money his honesty was never questioned. Notwithstanding his forever-recurring caprices and changes, his principles were high, always high, and absolutely unshakable.
>
> He was the strangest compound that ever got mixed in a human mold. Such a person as that is given to acting upon impulse and without reflection; that was Orion's way. Everything he did he did with conviction and enthusiasm and with a vainglorious pride in the thing he was doing—and no matter what that thing was, whether good, bad or indifferent, he repented of it every time in sackcloth and ashes before twenty-four hours had sped.

Pessimists are born, not made. Optimists are born, not made. But I think he was the only person I have ever known in whom pessimism and optimism were lodged in exactly equal proportions. Except in the matter of grounded principle, he was as unstable as water. . . . He was always truthful; he was always sincere; he was always honest and honorable. But in light matters — matters of small consequence, like religion and politics and such things — he never acquired a conviction that could survive a disapproving remark from a cat. (Mark Twain, *The Autobiography of Mark Twain* [New York: Washington Square Press, 1917], pp. 91–93.)

From the above description we might infer that Orion Clemens may have suffered from manic-depressive illness. Or, as I wish to suggest, he simply had powerful, inborn personality traits.

Our second sample is from an epic poem in which we find an eloquent statement of what a person is by birth and what the expectations of others force him to try to be. It is taken from Dante's *Divine Comedy*, "Paradiso," Canto 8, the headnote to which reads in part: "Dante asks how it is that mean sons can be born of great fathers, and Charles [of Anjou] answers with a discourse on the diversity of natural talents . . . for only by diversity of gifts can society function. Not only does God provide for the diversities of every nature, but for their good and harmony beside. God had planned these variations to a harmonious end. Mankind, by forcing men into a situation not in harmony with their talents, strays from God's plan." So the king asks:

> "Would man be worse off than he is,
>   there on earth, without a social order?"
> "Yes!" I replied, "nor need I proof of this."
> "And can that be, unless men there below
>   lived variously to serve their various functions?
>
> . . . .
>   Your various aptitudes,
>   it follows, therefore, must have various roots,
> So one man is born Xerxes and another Solon;
>   one Melchizedek, and another he
>   who, flying through the air, lost his own son.
> That ever-revolving nature whose seal is pressed
>   into our mortal wax does its work well,
>   but takes no heed of where it comes to rest.

So Esau parted from Jacob in the seed:
     And Romulus was born of such humble stock
     that Mars became his father as men agreed.
Begotten and begetter, but for the force
     of overruling Providence, the son's nature
     would always follow in the father's course.

. . . .

What nature gives a man Fortune must nourish
     concordantly, or nature, like any seed
     out of its proper climate, cannot flourish.
If the world below would learn to heed the plan
     of nature's firm foundation and build on that,
     it would have the best from every man.
But into Holy Orders you deflect
     the man born to strap on a sword and shield,
     and make a King of one whose intellect
     is given to writing sermons. And, in this way
     your footprints leave the road and go astray."
(Dante Alighieri, *The Divine Comedy*, trans. John
Giardi [New York: W. W. Norton and Company,
1970], Paradiso, Canto 8:1.)

The two foregoing examples, one a brother's impression and
one a poetic observation of the human race, vividly describe unreconciled inborn personality and learned character.

To understand reconciliation, consider the homey trait of shyness. Emerging research suggests that shyness in some people may
be an inborn personality trait. "One possible explanation of individual differences in shyness is heredity; shyness may be a personality trait with a substantial genetic component. If so, shyness
should be classified as a basic personality temperament."
(Jonathan M. Cheek, Alan B. Zonderman, "Shyness as a Personality Temperament," paper presented at the American Psychology
Association symposium, Anaheim, California, August 1983. See
also Michael F. Pogue-Geile and Richard J. Rose, "Developmental
Genetic Studies of Adult Personality," *Developmental Psychology*, 1985, vol. 21, no. 3, pp. 547–57; Catherine M. Busch,
"Evaluating Comprehensiveness in Personality Systems: The
California Q-Set and Five Factor Mode," *Journal of Personality*,
vol. 54, no. 2, June 1986, pp. 430–46.)

Otis was shy. If late for a college class, he would skip the class rather than enter the room. Public speaking, when he was coerced into it, made him physically ill. Yet the facts of life faced him: he had to go to class to earn a college degree, and his mind stirred with ideas that he hoped were worth expressing, even if a speech was the effective method. So Otis signed up for speech. He also learned to go to classes early the first week or two of the semester to get formally assigned to a seat near the back door of each classroom. Eventually Otis developed into an adequate speaker. And he remained shy even throughout his two-year mission for the Church.

After his mission Otis married an outgoing woman. As they enhanced their relationship he learned to defer to her in social settings. She in turn became sensitive to his reticence and carried the conversation in many situations. Otis learned to be such an effective listener that he was eventually able to offer a sincere listening ear for considerable stretches. It could be said of Otis now that he is effective in most relationships because he understands his basic personality and he has developed character traits that reconcile with it.

In contrast, a pertinent example of the destructive power of raw, unreconciled personality was revealed by the testimony of forger and murderer Mark Hoffman. The man had certain innate abilities. It was a tragedy that he did not develop character traits by which to channel his personality into benevolent activities.

Hoffman forged several "historical" documents that allegedly pertained to the origins of The Church of Jesus Christ of Latter-day Saints. In earlier years he had participated in the usual orthodox character-shaping experiences afforded by active membership in the Church, but he permitted his personality to override his character. He concocted documents that, had they been genuine, would have threatened to undermine the authenticity of the Church itself. He fleeced several people of many thousands of dollars. He murdered at least two people. All this, when it was finally revealed, appeared inexplicable to outside observers.

Hoffman himself supplied the explanation in terms such as we are using in this chapter. He is quoted as saying: "It's hard for a lot of people to accept, I'm sure, that my closest friends and even my wife did not know the extent of my fraudulent dealings. But those people do not know my personality. In other words, I have always been fairly introverted. I have never had really close friends that I've shared information with." (*Mark Hoffman Interviews, Vol. 2,* Office of the Salt Lake County Attorney, April 1987, p. 421.)

This case makes a dark point. We place such great emphasis on what others do to the child during the early formative years that we neglect to evaluate how the child acts and reacts during this period. How young Mark Hoffman was raised is certainly pertinent. But just as pertinent is how he reacted to being raised. It seems most likely that during the formative years his parents tried to teach him decent concern for other people. Yet by his own testimony he was unresponsive. This comes through in chilling tones as one reads the 537 pages detailing his campaign to destroy faith, defraud, rob, and murder.

The theory that parents can completely shape the child's character is indefensible. It implies an absolute influence that no parent ever has. Indeed, when total control is attempted, children either rebel or collapse into utter dependence. And whatever may be his external reactions, no one controls the child's inner thoughts. Countless parents droop under the deadly belief that they have ruined their child. Actually, such power is not given parents by the normal laws of nature or God.

True, extreme abuse can devastate a child's heart, for there is no disputing that parental love is one of life's most urgent needs. In fact the truly heroic stories in all cultures tell of the sacrifices parents make for their children. But unreserved love for a child is not the same as assuming responsibility for everything that the child does or becomes. Within the usual range of parent-child relations, parents ultimately can influence behavior only as much as the child permits. Within a loving home environment — or even a harsh one — the child makes many choices. It was so in our premortal home, and the law has never been repealed. It is erroneous, even cruel, to expect of mere earthly parents coercive powers that our eternal parents refused to exercise, powers of such magnitude that a war was fought in heaven over them:

And I, the Lord God, spake unto Moses, saying: That Satan, whom thou hast commanded in the name of mine Only Begotten, is the same which was from the beginning, and he came before me saying—Behold, here am I, send me, I will be thy son, and I will redeem all mankind, that one soul shall not be lost, and surely I will do it; wherefore give me thine honor.

But, behold, my Beloved Son, which was my Beloved and Chosen from the beginning, said unto me—Father, thy will be done, and the glory be thine forever.

Wherefore, because that Satan rebelled against me, and sought to destroy the agency of man, which I, the Lord God, had given him, and also, that I should give unto him mine own power; by the power of mine Only Begotten, I caused that he should be cast down.

And he became Satan, yea, even the devil, the father of all lies, to deceive and to blind men, and to lead them captive at his will, even as many as would not hearken unto my voice. (Moses 4:1–4.)

To understand ourselves, then, we need to know which past choices we have made and which have been made for us by other people, particularly our parents. And which choices—ours or theirs—clash with our personalities. We have free will or agency. Its expression is an extension of personality. Express it we must. Others, especially parents, react. If they react with patient benevolence and gently but firmly teach us good character traits, we ought to count ourselves blessed. If they are harsh, disapproving, or abusive, we are at risk. Some of us reject loving parents' values. Some of us overcome abusive parents' values. Either way, we react by the God-given right of agency.

Social scientists recognize this agency, though not as a heavenly gift.

The process begins very early. Parents do not react to a happy, responsive infant in the same way that they react to a fretful or unresponsive one. An active, venturesome child has a greater variety of experiences than a more passive or timorous one. This is called active gene-environment correlation. . . .

Most important of all is *active* gene-environment correlation, the child's own tendency to seek out experiences compatible with his or her genetic proclivities. Many personality traits, such as social potency, can be observed in nursery school, where some children are already developing the habits and skills that will make them into socially effective adults. Both the impulsive child and the cautious, controlled child are rewarded for approaching life in the ways that are natural to them. The impulsive child learns to expect variety and unpredictability in experience, and to accept the attendant misfortunes. The cautious child learns to expect a more predictable environment and to fear the unfamiliar. (David T. Lykken, "Genes and the Mind," The Harvard Medical School Mental Health Letter, vol. 14, no. 2, August 1987, p. 6.)

Here is the nub of the matter. A child may be, by nature, cautious and wary. If this is an inborn personality trait, especially one that was acquired in the life prior to this earthly one, then attempts by self or others to extinguish such traits can and do cause confusion.

To reconcile our personality and character is to reach an internal peace about who and what we have been, are now, and intend to become. This opens the way for self-understanding and for healing of troubled relationships; for by bringing our personality and our character into harmony, we give others someone secure and predictable to relate to. And we are at peace with ourselves. This was the essence of Polonius's advice to Laertes about relationships:

> And these few precepts in thy memory
> See thou character. Give thy thoughts no tongue,
> Nor any unproportion'd thought his act.
> Be thou familiar, but by no means vulgar.
> Those friends thou hast, and their adoption tried,
> Grapple them to thy soul with hoops of steel;
>
> . . . .
>
> Beware
> Of entrance to a quarrel; but, being in,
> Bear't that the opposed may beware of thee.
> Give every man thine ear, but few thy voice;
> Take each man's censure, but reserve thy judgment.
>
> . . . .
>
> This above all, —to thine own self be true;
> And it must follow, as the night the day,
> Thou canst not then be false to any man.
> (Shakespeare, *Hamlet*, Act 1, scene 3.)

Part of us —personality —is so embedded that to tamper with it can confuse us, for we came from a home before mortality where love suffused all relationships. To have one's personality twisted and wrenched is wounding. To comprehend this damage, watch closely a little child of three or less. What would be the effect on him if his ingenuous, spontaneous interests and expressions were jeered at or punished? What terror envelops a wary child who is forced into frightening situations? Conversely what joy brightens innocent eyes when little arms reach out and the child is lifted up to be cuddled and kissed?

An emerging specialty in child behavioral research focuses on "resilient" children. These are children who, despite growing up in bad situations —dangerous neighborhoods, poverty, divorced parents, inadequate early education — rebound and move ahead to lead productive, healthy lives while others with similar backgrounds disintegrate. A growing body of data gives insight as to why these children emerge strong while others are wounded for life. No single factor accounts for resilience, but some are more significant than others; for example, the encouragement of a loving relative or mentor during bleak periods.

Another strong factor is childhood "competence," or success at various tasks during the formative years. These episodes of success appear to be far more significant than the downward pressures of negative environments. One study of boys over a period of forty years into their adult years found that competence in certain areas led to enriched human relationships. These areas included regular part-time jobs, regular household chores, involvement in extracurricular activities at school, strong grades relative to their intellectual capacity, and coping capacity. (See J. Kirk Felsman, George E. Vaillant, "Resilient Children as Adults: A 40-Year Study," in *The Invulnerable Child*, eds. E. J. Anthony and B. Cohler [New York: Guilford Press, 1987].)

It is this factor of "coping capacity" that has particular bearing on our discussion, for it seems to be an inner, innate, unlearned trait; unlearned at least in this life, since it asserts itself in the child's reaction to his or her situation too early and too consistently to be learned after birth. The Felsman-Vaillant article states (p. 305): "We are finding courageous individuals who have demonstrated long-term patterns (including periods of limitation and setback) of continued mastery and competence, despite the multiple factors working against them. It is the sustained maintenance of these characteristics in the face of enormous odds that distinguishes them from their peers."

These resilient people are not carefree and blissful. They carry scars. They know sorrow and despair. But despite all they have undergone, they persist. By force of will they suppress rather than repress. They are conscious of the bad things they have experienced, but instead of descending into cynicism they have a remarkable empathy for the struggles of other people. "What, if anything, sets them apart is that despite enormous odds, their lives reveal a clear pattern of recovery, restoration, and gradual mastery" (p. 311).

To account for such resilience in biological terms is mundanely adequate, but such attitudes are elevated to eternal significance if attributed to a life decisively lived as intelligent, agentive spirit persons and personalities prior to this mortality. How the knowledge acquired premortally is passed on through the spirit to the physical body is far beyond my ability to comprehend. That there exists such a phenomenon is indisputable. The reconciliation between character building here and this premortally acquired personality is a rigorous, life-long, and noble quest.

I was privileged to watch the remarkable rebirth of a seventy-year-old woman as she reconciled her personality and character. Her pure white hair and fine features gave her a noble demeanor. She had given years of service to family, friends, and church, but she had never been at peace. She was quite apologetic for anything she did, despite her many exceptional talents.

Finally, worn down by inner warfare, she let the truth come out: Her high-spirited personality in childhood had clashed with her mother's preferences for tight emotional control. Rather severe punishments eventually convinced the youngster that she was, if not wicked, at best rude, offensive, and undesirable. And for the next fifty-five years she tried to convince herself that such was the case. But the personality, which she brought with her from before birth, would not be extinguished.

Only the wonder at watching an imprisoned spirit breaking free so late in life outweighed the sadness I felt because so fine a soul had suffered so long—not just from a misguided mother's errors, but also from her own decision to accept other people's definitions of her. And, as one might expect, as she came to peace within herself her relationships became even deeper and finer than before.

Erikson reflected on this:

> I'm convinced that old people and children need one another and that there's an affinity between old age and childhood that, in fact, rounds out the life cycle. You know, old people often seem childlike, and it's important that we be permitted to revive some qualities that we had as children. . . . Einstein used the word "wonder" to describe his experience as a child, and he was considered childlike by many people. . . . He claimed that he was able to formulate the theory of Relativity because he kept asking the questions that children ask. So when I say old people think like children, I do not mean childishly, but with wonder, joy, playfulness—all those things that adults often have to sacrifice for a while. (Elizabeth Hall, "A Conversation with Erik Erikson," *Psychology Today*, June 1983, p. 24.)

Would it be consistent with scripture and revelation to infer that personality traits gained during the premortal experience could be beneficial to relationships in mortality? If this is the case, each person born can consider herself or himself as *good* at birth, as having accomplished significant growth before birth:

"For the word of the Lord is truth, and whatsoever is truth is light, and whatsoever is light is Spirit, even the Spirit of Jesus Christ. And the Spirit giveth light to every man that cometh into the world." (D&C 84:45–46.)

"Every spirit of man was innocent in the beginning; and God having redeemed man from the fall, men became again, in their infant state, innocent before God" (D&C 93:38; see also, Charles R. Harrell, "The Development of the Doctrine of Preexistence, 1830–1844," in *BYU Studies*, vol. 28, no. 2, Spring 1988, pp. 74–96).

Even our meager knowledge of premortal life suggests a diversity of attributes and characteristics among the spirits there (see Abraham 3:22–23, 28). If this is a correct inference, the implications for self-understanding are considerable. For one thing, personal qualities brought from a timeless setting may translate into different shades of meaning in our time-governed environment. Instead of seeing the child (or ourselves) as stubborn or willful it may be more accurate to see the trait of perseverance. What some resent as uninhibited behavior may well be, from the eternal perspective, effervescence. The list will be as long as the myriad traits that make the human family a sparkling mosaic of diversity.

When inborn uniqueness is squelched, harm is done to the core, the identity, of the person. Such wounds can cripple that person's ability to establish and maintain relationships. Reconciliation of personality and character is the process that enriches or heals such wounds. By this a person is able to free himself of crushing self-doubt while at the same time setting out on the invigorating quest to define himself in the image of divinity.

Obviously, an inborn personality trait can become good or bad by the character traits we accumulate. Determination can become fanaticism. Contemplation can deteriorate into aimlessness. And so on.

Reconciliation of personality and character must not become an alibi for avoiding emotional investment in relationships. Acceptance of inborn traits is widespread in the human sciences. By attributing this solely to genetics some scientists worship DNA. Those whose faith is that all creation issues forth from the loving decrees of a Heavenly Father and his Son, kneel at a different altar. To them, God-given personal agency is to be used to initiate and nurture relationships of all kinds. The Savior is the model. Immutable law flows from the Father. The purifying influence is the Holy Ghost, so aptly named the Comforter. Development of character is the process of refining personality. Relationships founded upon these realities are profoundly different from others.

To comprehend these parts of ourselves and our relationship with the Godhead is elemental to self-understanding. By this we enhance ordinary relationships or heal troubled ones until they become sublime.

Summary

We need to embrace or rediscover those parts of us that are or were childlike. What made us joyful, playful, and wonder-struck as children? How did we show these traits? What key incidents happened to us to suppress them? You will recall that we discussed some of this in chapter 9 (on family relationships).

This is the ultimate self-definition, self-discipline, self-understanding—to remember who we were and to reconcile that with our present capacities by developing character traits that enhance or heal relationships.

Husbands, love your wives,
even as Christ also loved the
church, and gave himself for
it.
— Ephesians 5:25

Sexual Relationships

CHAPTER TWELVE

T here remains a facet of self-definition that has to be examined
by itself, for by its nature it affects our relationships with other
people. It is sex, its glories and vulgarities.

An exquisite truth has been revealed in the lives of those whom
I have seen gain sexual intimacy. It is that they have quietly, very
privately, developed a passion and enjoyment not documented in
the professional literature, let alone in the mass media, for it is an
outgrowth of their inner, separate reconciliation. It is not based
upon erotic performance. It is discrete yet joyous intimacy. And it
is an expression of covenants the couple have made with God to
respect the powers of life with which he has invested sexual expression.

There are numberless books, pamphlets, advertisements, and
popular media products devoted to sex. Frankly, I must confess to
a deep weariness of the subject as it is used to promote self-
focused, sensual gratification. In fact, if a person takes the time to

wade through the pop-sex manuals, and not a few of the sober, serious professional ones, he perceives that the treatment of the subject can become ludicrous.

The subjects we have dealt with in previous chapters are far more significant than sex. While sex *is* important, the sexual act can be merely hedonistic or even demeaning. It takes little or no empathy to "pet" or to have sexual intercourse. Eroticism is probably the lowest common denominator in human relations, because it requires only appetite, the opportunity to gratify appetite, and the ability to perform the act. Its demands on the intellect and the heart are low. It creates no enduring commitments when it is the sole basis of a relationship. Sexual activity without rules and without relationships harms individuals and societies. If it becomes an end in itself it recognizes no restraints, respects no privacy, and destroys the sanctity of home and person. Certainly, unbridled gratification of this appetite is an enemy of human relationships.

Marriage is the context within which this chapter addresses sexual relationships. Acquaintance with people who have been damaged by premarital and extramarital sexual encounters has purged me of any personal or professional illusions about their purported excitements. The popular media make millions of dollars by selling sex outside of marriage. In doing this they blatantly disregard human beings who are emotionally damaged by sex without commitment. Single adults may claim a right to sexual satisfaction, but their claims cannot obliterate the sorrow of people who are wounded by sex without relationships, without meaning, without respect. It is one thing to claim the right to whole and wholesome relationships and quite another to demand orgasmic license.

There is a terrible arrogance to the sophistic claim that sex, one of mankind's strongest urges and enjoyments, can be performed casually or promiscuously without detrimental consequences. Yet observation of people who have gone from sexual distress to sexual fulfillment demonstrates that this aspect of human relationships is indeed every bit as powerful as poets and lovers have claimed, and that it can either degrade or enrich a relationship.

Knowing people whose lives testify to the sorrows or joys of sexual activity has confirmed my conviction that it is best enjoyed as God intended it to be, by people who nurture each other within a strong, committed marriage. When it is used as a way to get selfish erotic or emotional gratification, even within a legal marriage, it harms those involved. And, as important as a lover's technique may be, kindness, pleasant humor, and respect are the true ingredients of passion.

There are as many approaches to this subject as there are sexual practices. Our earlier categorization of relationships — civil, affectionate, and intimate — should serve us usefully here.

Sexual Civility

Civility in sexuality these days has been shunted aside by a misguided reaction against what is erroneously called "old-fashioned ideas" of courtship. In their zeal to justify premarital sex, too many sexologists have failed to comprehend what cultural anthropologists have so thoroughly documented: cultural norms and rituals for sexual behaviors often are of great value to sound relationships. Those civilities that used to permeate courtship in Western cultures laid a very useful foundation for the marital relationship.

Of those marriages that I have known that might be termed good, *all* have one factor in common. They either courted each other before marriage or learned to during the marriage. They say please and thank you, and seem to look for ways to make their spouses' lives brighter. Criticism is minimal if it occurs at all. Grooming and hygiene are important to them; daily bathing, use of deodorant, fresh breath, fresh clothing. These people listen to their spouses. They anticipate their spouses' wishes as much as possible. They tolerate and encourage and, when it is in the best interest of their spouses, they challenge. They do not cave in to unreasonable demands. They give and expect respect.

Do these belong to a rare species of idealists that knows little pressure, is well-to-do, and is, if the truth were known, avoiding reality? Not at all. These folks have disagreements and dislikes, and they experience the stresses that harm other marriages. They have learned, however, that simple civility enriches a relationship.

Civility in sexual acts begins with respect for the other person's body, mind, and spirit. Is there any uglier presumption than that a woman is a convenience to be exploited at the whim of a man? Or is it an improvement to urge women to adopt the aggressions and demands that men have been taught are their conjugal right?

Civility must include an effort to learn about and honor the other's thoughts and values about sex. It is necessary for newly-weds (and "oldlyweds") to talk about sex. They must, for their own sakes, discuss their respective values, the family norms they bring to the marriage, what they know about the body, what discomfort they fear, what practices seem desirable and what seem unpleasant.

In every marriage there ought to be discussions of important matters. No man or woman ought to accept as healthy a relation-ship in which one partner refuses to discuss important aspects of the couple's future together. Nowhere is it written in good science or good religion that a wife must submit herself sexually to a hus-band who will not at least listen to and respond to her values about their sexual life. Many marital problems would be pre-vented or healed if the spouses — often the women — would firmly require proper attention to what they considered important in matters of relationships. Almost any marriage counselor can write a book about couples who elected to suffer years of distress rather than talk to each other. One of the most perplexing behavioral syndromes occurs between spouses who share each other's bodies intimately yet cannot discuss the experience. By talking, couples can prevent or solve problems. As a simple example, one young wife who enjoyed full sexual expression told her husband that it was also enjoyable just to be hugged in bed some nights.

Among the saddest tales are those of couples who failed to share with each other the fact that one (or even both) was sexually abused in childhood. Hence years of misunderstanding went by that could have been prevented by this sharing.

Values about what practices are right and wrong, pleasant or offensive, need civil airing. This delicate process calls for the ut-most respect.

More than one marriage has been weakened for years by inci-vility on the honeymoon. A couple had traveled some distance from the wedding reception, and both had perspired heavily. After showering and grooming herself, the newly married young woman came out into the motel room. Her husband, who was watching a video cassette on a rented machine, had not changed his clothes nor showered since the day began sixteen hours earlier. Glancing up, he abruptly asked why she still had on her nightgown. For the rest of the honeymoon he was just as inconsiderate.

From that disillusioning night, resentment grew within the wife's heart. Years later, as she was struggling to stay in the marriage, she had to admit that his crude, uncivil behavior on the honeymoon was no different from his behavior before. When I asked why she had tolerated it, she gave an answer I have heard far too often: "Because I thought he would change when we got married." This expectation is an illusion. There are very few men or women who are unpleasant during courtship, only to turn nice afterwards. Almost always our behavior prior to marriage reveals the inner person — even when we are on our *best* behavior. A sufficiently long and varied courtship usually shows us at our best and worst.

Then there are people who are naive. One couple sought my help the morning after their wedding night because they had failed to consummate the marriage. She had been unable to relax enough to grant him entry. He refused to risk hurting her, so they spent a mutually anxious night contemplating the ocean outside their room. The solution was rather simple: he was not taking enough time to caress and arouse her; she was not informing him of this. By seeking correct information promptly the next day, they were able to relieve the frustration and pain of temporary vaginismus by the next night.

Each of the incidents cited up to this point could have been civilly discussed before sexual activities were attempted, or soon after. Whether or not couples have foresight, there is a particularly sweet experience available to those who lie in each other's arms and talk about what they have just experienced or wish to enjoy. Such talk is not coldly clinical or vulgar. It is the private, civil consideration of two lovers within the sanctity of marriage, who are being considerate not to injure each other spiritually or physically.

It is not unusual for one spouse to be more comfortable about talking than the other. This is the utility of civility. If one spouse conveys feelings about certain practices and does so gently, without threat and without requiring an intense dialogue, the more reticent spouse can listen and digest at his own pace. This also means that one expects to be treated civilly. Each one kindly but firmly corrects the other's mistakes. Each clearly rejects repeated uncivil treatment, nipping it in the bud lest it become a habit.

Sexual Affection

Affection, the next phase of marital sexuality, eludes many people, unfortunately. The powerful images of television and movies have taught an entire generation that boy meets girl, boy takes girl to bed. Or, in the latest version, girl takes boy to bed. Far too many couples go from the civil phase to lustful erotic activity without developing the affectionate portion of the relationship.

Depending on their value system, some people marry so as to legitimize sexual behavior but little affection is involved. Or, doing what they believe is their right as consenting adults having biologic imperatives, they indulge in unmarried, affectionless sex. As one college professor observed, "When I see a young couple who have lived together throughout their college years leave each other with a handshake and move out into life, I am struck dumb" (Allan Bloom, *The Closing of the American Mind* [New York: Simon and Schuster, 1987], p. 123).

Various worrisome sexual patterns are emerging in our society. Among unmarried adolescents sex is practiced as a game without affection. There has even evolved a sexual dysfunction called disorders of sexual desire in which healthy people lose interest in sex. (See Helen Singer Kaplan, *Disorders of Sexual Desire* [New York: Brunner / Mazel, 1979].)

Does this mean that sexual pleasure is overrated? Hardly. The point is that there is more to the matter than the physical act alone. People who begin their marital relationship on a firm foundation usually are quite affectionate. For them, affection is both a test and a treat before they engage in sexual activities. As they test the possibilities of the relationship, they come to know whether there is pleasure in simply touching hands and talking, in spending time together in cultural or recreational pursuits. They discover whether they can attend church, worship, and pray together with unity of purpose. If they are Latter-day Saints, she learns whether he honors the priesthood; he learns whether she is true to her covenants.

There is danger in lack of emotional and physical affection. Refusing to talk or touch affectionately can be symptoms of major immaturity or even pathological disorder. Affectionate thoughts and actions, without the goal of seduction, enable two people to gradually learn how to enjoy each other. Where do you touch someone when you want to reassure them, to add to their self-esteem? Why do women seem to be spontaneously affectionate and men so inhibited? What are words of endearment? Where and when does a person learn how to express affection? Working out the answers to such questions can enhance the relationship.

Time and again I have struggled to help husbands learn the arts of affection *after* they have nearly driven their wives away. Their sexual relationships were adequate if measured by erotic competence. What they lacked was affection. At the time of crisis, many of these men reacted similarly: frantic at the discovery that their marriages were nearly dead, they became extremely intense in trying to salvage them and, mistaking intensity for affection, drove their wives further away with overwhelming attentions. A more promising solution is to be affectionate, neither demeaning oneself nor pandering to the spouse.

Warren was male chauvinism personified. His incessant put-downs had leached out of his wife any emotional energy. Judy's every word and act was deliberate and measured so as to avoid provoking his demeaning remarks. Courtesy did not exist for them. Sex was an obligation for Judy, a right for Warren.

Warren was not physically cruel or aggressive; rather, he was self-focused. The world and all its inhabitants revolved around him. Although Warren had been confronted by a professional counselor about his unkind tongue and had moderated some of his remarks, he still treated sex as a technique, a way to release his tensions, and one of his rights as a husband. He flatly stated that he had never thought about the larger issue of intimacy. Now, faced with an ailing marriage, he was willing to reexamine the purpose of sexual activity.

At this point he read a book about social, emotional, and spiritual intimacy. Some time afterward, Warren and Judy had sexual intercourse. At their next counseling session, Judy said that it had been the most enjoyable sexual experience of their married life.

Asked why, she replied that Warren had treated her as if he cared for her; he had been affectionate.

This was no erotic breakthrough. Warren was not suddenly a skillful lover. Judy was still reserved. Even so, Warren's efforts to be affectionate conveyed something reassuring to his long-suffering wife. It did not cure all of their problems by any means, but it did enable these two people to begin to enjoy one another as never before.

Sex without an affectionate relationship is stale, episodic, and puerile. And sex, even within a rich relationship—*especially* within a rich relationship—is a a subordinate part.

A type of affectionless marital sexual trauma is increasing among young people whose values condemn premarital intercourse but whose behavior prior to marriage includes everything else but that. Before marriage these unwise people experiment with various forms of mutual eroticism, from mild petting to orgasmic stimulation, but stop short of full genital intercourse. They "make out" or "pet" or "fool around." In short, they lust for erotic gratification. This can lead to a classic conditioned response: Having learned arousal and self-focused climax without affection, or without concern for the partner's needs, after marriage they find intercourse itself unsatisfying. And they belatedly discover that they have little or no affectionate relationship.

The great danger of premarital petting is that it is a game, an exciting one that is encouraged by innumerable movies and television shows. But being a game it cheapens true sexual affection and intimacy, for it permits the participants to experience exotic physical sensations utterly devoid of spiritual enhancement in the relationship. Petting is to marital intimacy as rock music is to the Hallelujah Chorus; it stirs one's adrenalin but not one's soul.

A husband and wife can embrace, kiss, and caress with the affectionate intention of giving pleasure. This enjoyment has been given the unfortunate label of foreplay. I find this objectionable for two reasons: it implies irreversible arousal, and it devalues sexual pleasures that do not always include genital activity and orgasm. Warmly massaging your wife's weary back can have sexual meaning, as can kissing her or caressing her in ways and places she finds desirable. But it need go no further if she is tired or distracted. The gift you present by doing this is affection of a very pleasurable kind, affection that reassures and relaxes as, for a moment, it causes the stresses of the world to subside.

Let us be reminded of the connection between overall affection and sexual affection. Draw your own conclusions about the quality of the honeymoon relationship of the couple in the following fiftieth anniversary vignette.

> Irene and Eddie Reiss of Camarillo proved that, to make a marriage work, it pays to use your noodle. . . . For their honeymoon, Eddie, who was a bread truck driver, took the next day off.
>
> "We shopped for groceries, we took in a movie, and then we went back to our apartment for the first meal she would be preparing for me," Eddie said.
>
> "I had asked him what he liked," Irene said, "and he replied that he liked noodles. I bought some, but I had never cooked any before."
>
> She proceeded to put a pound of raw noodles into a small saucepan. "Everything began boiling over," she said. "There were noodles on the stove, noodles on the floor, and even some remained in the pan—half raw.
>
> "I wanted to throw the whole mess out, but he insisted that I serve it, and with each bite he kept saying how delicious it tasted."
>
> To this day, Irene, 71, is still impressed: "How could you not stay with a man like that 50 years?" (David Larson, "The Secret of Marriage: Going for the Gold," *Los Angeles Times,* 12 February 1988, part V, p. 11.)

One marriage began to die when, during the honeymoon, the husband impulsively pinched his wife's breast. The physical hurt was minor compared to the insult. She harbored unspoken resentment; he was too dull to inquire. By the end of the week the relationship was dying.

In contrast, another couple did not engage in sexual intercourse for two or three days after their wedding because they wanted to learn other things about each other first. They were affectionate during that time. In preparation for marriage they had sought advice about the very things we are considering here. Highly educated, each of them worked in technical fields at the time of their marriage. Each had had traumatic emotional experiences earlier with other people. As they later reflected on their honeymoon, they felt that by enjoying non-sexual affection before they attempted physical intercourse they were prepared to appreciate a dimension of physical enjoyment that otherwise could have been overlooked.

The author Ernest K. Gann put affection and marriage in perspective. Before he wrote his bestselling novel *The High and the Mighty*, he had sold the screen rights of an earlier book. While in Hollywood, working as a consultant during the filming, he stayed with a couple he had known from earlier and humbler days, Jim and Jane Gainer. Late one night Gann returned to the Gainers' modest bungalow, flushed with the heady experiences of a Hollywood day. He hoped the Gainers were still up so he could "share [his] extraordinary news."

> I was about to call out . . . when I had halted suddenly and stood in awe. For in crossing the room I had detoured around the coffee table and so changed my angle of perception. Now I could not avoid seeing into the bedroom and the scene within drove all other thoughts from me. Jim's long frame was stretched beneath the bed covers, his head propped on a pillow. He was reading a book . . . Jane Gainer was on her knees beside the bed, her nightgown making her seem as small and frail as a newly hatched bird. Her head was bent in prayer, and her hands were clutched on the edge of the bed.
>
> I could hear no sound until Jim sighed heavily and reaching out with his free hand felt the air above his wife a moment, then lowered his hand to pat her gently on the head. Not once did he glance at her. . . .
>
> I tiptoed away, passing through the kitchen in darkness until I came to my little room at the back of the bungalow. And I thought I should have been ashamed of my Peeping Tom conduct, but I was not.
>
> Rich man? Yes I was, just in being able to tiptoe past my good friends' marvelous treasury. (Ernest K. Gann, *A Hostage to Fortune* [New York: Alfred A. Knopf, 1978], p. 305.)

Sexual Intimacy

Over the years people knowing of my work but not seeking professional help have discreetly shared insights into their sexual intimacy. None have given graphic descriptions. Other people who were seeking professional help have also discussed their sexual intimacies. There is, of course, extensive professional literature on sexual attitudes and behaviors. And there are diaries, journals, and letters that can be drawn upon. These various sources taken together form the basis of this part of this chapter.

The quality of sexual intimacy varies with mood and circumstance. Sexual expression can be an offering of respect or it can be the meanest of insults. Those who understand this appear to know the difference between the "rights" and the "rites" of marriage. These people have learned, often through trial and error, that ultimate sexual communion consists of sacred rites which renew, reaffirm, and refine. They honor the body and its parts and its senses. A gentle sense of humor lightens the moods. They do not use pornography or gutter terms or mechanical devices. Neither is there anything prissy about their interests and enjoyments. They *are* passionate —but disciplined!

The wedding ceremony grants husband and wife conjugal *rights* to each other's body. Faithful love transforms marital sexuality into *rites* of intimacy. Through sexual intercourse life is either literally or symbolically created and the Giver of Life is honored.

Among the deeper wounds inflicted on the human heart has been the trivialization of sexual communion. The wounds are called by myriad names: "The joys of sex," "recreational sex," "doing your thing," "the sexual revolution," "the double standard," "give him what every man needs," "if you love me you'll show it." These are words of affliction, not of healing or enrichment.

In the way we are considering sexuality and as practiced by those who seem to achieve remarkable harmony, sexual intimacy includes sexual intercourse as well as that which prepares for and follows it. Sexual intimacy does not make either spouse the property of the other. Self-definition and self-discipline mean that neither husband nor wife feels obligated to satisfy demeaning demands by a spouse. To the contrary, it means that a spouse can expect decent, enjoyable sexual respect and passion. Thus we see how important civility and affection are to intimacy.

One family's oral history passed down through three generations a roughhewn rancher ancestor's morning ritual. At the start of every summer day, on his wife's pillow the devoted husband placed a fresh flower. In another family there is a business executive who prepares Saturday breakfast for his wife and serves it to her in bed. One of the hardest driving insurance salesmen around becomes like a bashful schoolboy when his wife even telephones him. A renowned church, government, and financial leader, when he saw his wife enter the room, exclaimed, "There's Sally," and left a group of men in mid-sentence. These husbands understand themselves enough to give affection. Sexual intimacy is a natural expression of how they revere their wives.

William Gladstone (1809–1898) of Great Britain, was Queen Victoria's prime minister four times. He was considered by many to be the greatest Western statesman of the nineteenth century. In his journal he recorded the difficulty his wife, Catherine, had in nursing their babies. She had a tendency toward breast infections that blocked the flow of milk. This not only deprived the little ones of nourishment but also caused Catherine great pain. Gladstone's matter-of-fact journal entries record that he frequently massaged Catherine's aching breasts. During one period in 1842 from October through December he ministered to her needs almost nightly, often throughout the night.

Later when Catherine was sore again trying to nurse their fifth child, her husband "rubbed a little for her, almost the first office I have been able to perform about her."

Gladstone's use of the term *office* bears upon our discussion. It refers, according to the dictionary, to a "religious or social ceremonial observance," a "rite" or "something done for another."

With the sixth child the problem recurred. The faithful husband administered "a long rubbing at night . . . and prayers as usual," until the mother's milk began to flow. (Peter Gay, *Education of the Senses*, vol. 1 of *The Bourgeois Experience: Victoria to Freud* [New York: Oxford University Press, 1984], p. 353.)

What total intimacy these journal entries reveal as a prominent, busy statesman lays aside all else, including his own sexual desires, to relieve his wife of her distress! And she, with understanding, gratefully accepts his attentions. What does this convey to later generations whose political candidates spar with the press about whether a man's marital infidelities reveal anything about his character? How utterly sterile seems "recreational sex" when contrasted to the sublime scene where a husband tends to his wife that she might nurture their children. Can there be a finer passion?

This is not to underestimate the sexual intimacy in which husband and wife share each other's bodies. The people I know who enjoy such a relationship find most sex manuals offensive, and often primitive. These people are discovering each other. They are not following some erotic road map created by strangers. They do not depend upon a route that dictates steps one through eight. And perhaps most significant of all, each seeks to enhance the other's enjoyment; their own enjoyment being a result of what they give.

These people understand themselves and can enjoy the powers of their bodies. They are mature enough to ask, to listen, to comment. Respect causes them to learn words and touches that increase their spouse's self-esteem. They are careful to be clean and fresh. They create those intimate rituals unique to their own relationship that are consistent with their values. They do not try bizarre experiments, although some were curious enough in their early marriage to explore a bit. In their spiritual and emotional maturity they do not offend, nor would they tolerate offensiveness.

Just as they are not ashamed of their bodies, neither do they take them for granted. They report that modesty is important to them. They do not wander about the house naked. Yet they appreciate and enjoy special moments of full intimacy with no barriers between them.

These people seem to understand the covenant of life that God offered to Adam and Eve when they discovered the sexuality of their bodies. Their response was to sew fig leaf aprons (Genesis 3:7) to cover their procreative parts, not from shame but from an awakened respect for the Godlike powers these represented. Adam admitted that when he heard God's voice calling he was afraid because of his nakedness. Why the fear? Not because they were unclothed, for in fact they were wearing modest aprons. Rather, the man and woman realized they had to confess to their Heavenly Father that they had been influenced by Satan's advice.

What happened next is usually interpreted according to the scripture reader's concept of fatherhood. Harsh mortal memories tend to make a person conjure up an angry God disgustedly expelling his naughty children from a pleasant home and condemning them to a miserable exile. Fortunately this version cannot with-

Christianity. The covenant is plain and simple. To begin with, the biblical account of Abraham and Sarah's conception of Isaac repudiates the erroneous charges that the Judeo-Christian heritage is pruddish and priggish. The token of the covenant was male circumcision, a symbol that anyone can understand. "This is my covenant, which ye shall keep, between me and you and thy seed after thee; every man child among you shall be circumcised" (Genesis 17:10).

It defies both revelation and reason to infer that a God who selected the male organ to symbolize his covenant was ashamed of the body part or its functions. But it is just as inconceivable to assume that he would be casual about the intimate parts of men and women who were created in his image, parts with which he endowed the power to create life. In scripture we find no silly jokes about sex. Prophets are not given to making smirking references to so normal and natural a function. As one scholar wryly noted, "Pious David . . . plies his [musical] instruments to the Glory of God—not, as do the Greek swains, merely for diversion or in order to sing 'amorous ditties all a summer's day' " (Theodor Gaster, *The Dead Sea Scriptures* [Garden City, N.Y.: Anchor Press, Doubleday, 1976], pp. 124–25).

Paul refers plainly to sexual organs as *vessels* and grants them a good place in God's plan.

"For this is the will of God, even your sanctification, that ye should abstain from fornication: that every one of you should know how to possess his vessel in sanctification and honour: not in the lust of concupiscence, even as the Gentiles which know not God" (1 Thessalonians 4:2–5).

The grandeur with which the scriptures invest marriage and its rites and sexual expression are captured by Paul's description of Abraham and Sarah. He speaks of them having faith to engage in sexual intercourse as required by God despite their advanced age. "And being not weak in faith, he considered not his own body now dead, when he was about an hundred years old, neither yet the deadness of Sara's womb. He staggered not at the promise of God through unbelief; but was strong in faith, giving glory to God; and being fully persuaded that, what he had promised, he was able also to perform. And therefore it was imputed to him for righteousness." (Romans 4:19–22.)

Paul connects Sarah's conception of Isaac with the promises of Jehovah, explaining that the mere act of sexual intercourse with the result of conception did not automatically pass along the blessings of the covenant. Fidelity to the covenant was required as well: "For they are not all Israel, which are of Israel: neither, because they are the seed of Abraham, are they all children: but, in Isaac shall thy seed be called. That is, they which are the children of the flesh, these are not the children of God: but the children of promise are counted for the seed." (Romans 9:6–8.)

Abraham and Sarah were chosen by God to demonstrate in a most singular way his covenant laws that sanctified not just marriage but the conception of life within marriage and the unbreakable obligation parents have to their children.

One commentator on the Dead Sea Scrolls stated: "Since the God of Melchizedek is expressly described as 'owner of heaven and earth,' the meaning is that Abraham will thenceforth have a stake in the things both of heaven on high and of the earth below. Moreover, since the priesthood in Israel and that of Melchizedek himself are said in Scripture to be eternal . . . it is not only to Abraham but also to his offspring that this privilege is vouchsafed; they will be linked to God in an everlasting covenant." (Theodor Gaster, *The Dead Sea Scriptures*, pp. 433–34.)

The rich nature of Abraham and Sarah's relationship as well as the candor of the ancient writers continue to elude the understanding of some modern minds. From a news magazine article on the Qumran community's writings comes this: "Most startling are new passages that record in great detail the physical beauty of Abraham's wife Sarah . . . [which are] proof that Judaic culture was not as puritanical or repressed as many scholars have suggested" (Philip Elmer deWitt, "When the Dead Are Revived," *Time*, 14 March 1988, p. 80).

The passages referred to are from the "Memoirs of the Patriarchs" and read in part: "How comely is the shape of her face, how . . . finespun are her tresses! How beautiful her eyes! How delicate is her nose and the whole lustre of her countenance! How fair are her breasts, and how comely withal is her complexion! . . . What is more, along with all this beauty she has great wisdom, and whatever she does turns out well." (Theodor Gaster, *The Dead Sea Scriptures*, p. 365.)

With mild prurient interest the modern newswriter emphasizes the erotic and sensual. This is in keeping with this generation's lustful fixation on the body, and on the female breasts in particular. The Bible refers plainly and often to women's breasts, but as sources of beauty and nurturance (see Proverbs 5:19; Job 3:12; Genesis 49:25). Unlike this modern writer, the scribe in Qumran was aware of both Sarah's attractiveness *and* her devotion to covenant sexual expression; for in the Qumran scrolls it was recorded that Sarah resisted the Pharaoh's advances for two years until he returned her, untainted, to her husband. (See Gaster, pp. 366–67.)

The Latter-day Saint is blessed to know with undeniable clarity the covenant nature of sexual capacity. On the one hand it is not to be used lustfully. "Thou shalt love thy wife with all thy heart, and shalt cleave unto her and none else. And he that looketh upon a woman to lust after her shall deny the faith, and shall not have the Spirit; and if he repents not he shall be cast out. Thou shalt not commit adultery; and he that committeth adultery, and repenteth not, shall be cast out." (D&C 42:22–24.)

On the other hand, when sanctified by priesthood ordinances and personal righteousness, sexual intimacy can be a power of godliness. A full explanation is contained in Doctrine and Covenants section 132. Consider the following excerpts:

For behold, I reveal unto you a new and an everlasting covenant; and if ye abide not that covenant, then are ye damned; for no one can reject this covenant and be permitted to enter into my glory. . . .

And again, verily I say unto you, if a man marry a wife by my word, which is my law, and by the new and everlasting covenant, and it is sealed unto them by the Holy Spirit of promise, by him who is anointed, unto whom I have appointed this power and the keys of this priesthood . . . it shall be done unto them in all things whatsoever my servant hath put upon them, in time and through all eternity; . . . and they shall pass by the angels, and the gods, which are set there, to their exaltation and glory in all things, as hath been sealed upon their heads, which glory shall be a fulness and a continuation of the seeds forever and ever. . . .

This promise is yours also, because ye are of Abraham, and the promise was made unto Abraham. (D&C 132:4, 19, 31.)

Can there be any other conclusion than that sexual activities at their finest are to be enjoyed only within marriage, and then as literal or symbolic rites of respect for their divine source? Rather than diminishing sexual intimacy, this knowledge has enriched the intimacy of those who include it in their relationships.

Such intimacy is decent, yet passionate. It is pleasurable, yet modest. It involves nothing degrading, demeaning, or painful. In the language of Genesis, "It is good." It is from the Creator who gave us the capacity to experience and to enjoy our senses. "Yea, all things which come of the earth [as does man himself from the dust], in the season thereof, are made for the benefit and the use of man, both to please the eye and to gladden the heart; yea, for food and for raiment, for taste and for smell, to strengthen the body and to enliven the soul" (D&C 59:18–19).

Summary

A man or a woman who desires to enrich or to heal a sexual relationship has to gain fundamental self-understanding about the values on which the relationship shall be based.

It could be said that even as a covenant couple express themselves sexually they are chaste by virtue of their fidelity to their marriage vows and their covenants with God. Failure to understand this leaves the relationship subject to the vagaries of shifting moods and circumstances. On the other hand, values that sustain civility and affection create a quality within which develops an intimacy marked by the finest marital relationships.

Love

CHAPTER THIRTEEN

Love concludes our journey. If this world and its relationships were purer we could just have written about and testified of love. Instead reality required that we offer the ideas and experiences of the preceding chapters. Our goal all along was love.

Let us conclude this book, then, by speaking of what relationships are like when people learn to love themselves and others. So as to convey the power of love, the examples given are of people who had to learn how to give and receive love.

Throughout history untold numbers of people have treated one another with love. "Behind the red facade of war and politics, misfortune and poverty, adultery and divorce, murder and suicide, were millions of orderly homes, devoted marriages, men and women kindly and affectionate, troubled and happy with children. Even in recorded history we find so many instances of goodness, even of nobility, that we can forgive, though not forget, the sins. The gifts of charity have almost equaled the cruelties of battlefields and jails. . . . Who will dare to write a history of human goodness?" (Will and Ariel Durant, *Lessons of History*, [New York: Simon and Schuster, 1968], p. 42.)

My mind roams over the lives of many people and recalls instance after instance of decency in the order that Jesus gave — love of God, neighbor, and self (see Matthew 22:35-40).

Love of Neighbor

Our Western civilization works because we have a *social contract* under which each of us is to do his part to make relationships at least civil. Terms of the social contract include obeying the law, respecting the other person's property, and not falsely yelling "Fire!" in a crowded theatre. These terms used to carry the great weight of tradition. They were possible because of shared values, most of which were derived from our Judeo-Christian heritage.

Occasionally the minimum contract is transcended by acts of great kindness. Strangers emulate the sublime parable of the Good Samaritan and rescue and succor other strangers.

Malcolm Muggeridge was with Mother Teresa as she performed her compassionate service in disease-infested Calcutta, India. She picked up one of the countless abandoned babies, this one found in a garbage can. " 'See,' she said, 'there is life in it!' So there was; and suddenly it was as though I were present at the Bethlehem birth, and the baby Mother Teresa was holding was another Lamb of God sent into the world to lighten our darkness." (Malcolm Muggeridge, *Jesus, the Man Who Lives* [London: Harper and Row, 1975], p. 29. See copyright and permission information, page 15 herein.)

A woman was brought into the mental hospital where I worked. She had stopped to eat at a modest café just off the freeway. While there she had a psychotic episode in which she behaved bizarrely and talked unintelligibly. The police were called, and they brought her to the hospital. For the rest of her two-week stay the owner of that café, a fellow who looked like his nondescript eating-place, visited her and brought her little gifts. He drove her car to the hospital. In the gloom cast by pervading mental illness this "Samaritan's" kindness was a beacon. It also taught one rookie social worker to look into people's souls rather than judge their outward appearance.

What is the significance of the Church's stated mission — to invite and help all to come unto Christ — but to love our neighbors as ourselves?

Love of Self

May I introduce the term *transition figure* here. It defines people who learn to love themselves so well that they provide a transition between generations. By their special love they enhance relationships as they heal wounds from previous generations and bless future ones.

The first time I recognized this in action is indelible in my memory. A very talented woman was contemplating divorcing her husband. After years of marriage, his unkindness and peculiar ways had worn her down until she feared that she was unattractive, incompetent, and just not worth much. Another man had expressed interest in her, which flattered her at a time when she was vulnerable. As we visited it was clear that she was painfully troubled at the thought of a divorce and its effect upon their several children.

In an attempt to strike to the core of her distress, and knowing that she took her marriage covenants seriously, I asked her how she felt the Savior, knowing of her husband's lonely childhood, would view him. What would Jesus expect of her at this time? I could see her wrestle with the question. Finally her face softened, and as if from the depths of her soul she whispered, "He would say, 'Oh, the poor man' and would love him." And from that moment she set out to love her husband as he had never been loved in his life.

This does not mean that she tolerated rudeness or abuse any longer. It does mean that she strove with all her might to see his virtues and applaud anything praiseworthy. He was, for example, a very diligent breadwinner, though of modest means. What she had undertaken was no small task, for she was battling generations of unexpressed affection in his background. A few years later she reported that theirs was a finer relationship than she had ever dared hope for.

The essential change that brought this about was her decision to be true to her covenants, to love with Christlike commitment. Out of this grew an unshakable love for herself, for she came to *know* that she was true to what she was convinced was eternal and holy. From being vulnerable to illicit romance she became invulnerably protected by her integrity. She became a transition figure, a person who healed troubled relationships from the past and let flow into her children's futures fidelity, affection, and love.

An exceptionally bright young man was raised in a home of hard-working, hard-drinking parents. The father's wages disappeared quickly as the unhappy man tried to dull his senses at the end of each futile workday. The family knew little of affection. The young man, however, set out with firm resolve to gain an education and establish himself in a high-prestige profession. This he did, and did exceptionally well, for in addition to a first-rate intellect he knew how to work, thanks to his parents. His greatest achievement was not professional, however. It was in overcoming a severe relationship crisis.

When he was about fifteen years into his marriage it was clear that his unrelenting drive to achieve professional and financial success had emotionally starved his wife and children. After some agonizing soul-searching he set out to learn to feel love and express it. He did not hide behind the cliché that he just could not express the love that was trapped within him. Nor did he claim that all he did was for his family's sake. Instead he admitted to himself that he knew precious little about love. Over the next two years he learned. He also learned how to express love. And the hardest person to love was himself. Because he loved others, he eventually was able to believe that he was worthy to be loved. And by this he became a transition figure.

Consider Beth's discovery of herself. It came midway in her struggle to heal many troubled relationships. She had already suffered more than twelve years of severe distress, and there were several more yet ahead. But she eventually achieved the victory. I believe the turning point was described in the following excerpt of a letter she wrote during the Christmas season.

> Well, here it is Christmas time again. I find we have all survived another year on this old earth. . . . We have grown and hopefully learned more of the lesson which Heavenly Father is teaching to help us that with Him we can conquer any trial. This year I

have come to one gigantic decision—I just do not wish to be married again. . . . I just feel content with my children. I'm capable of making decisions for them and myself and able to support them sufficiently and able to hire most anything else done. . . . I just don't care to please a man 24 hours a day 365 days a year anymore, especially when I never learned to do it without sacrificing my children's and my own needs first. I'm not bitter. I feel a calm, strange, peaceful contentment all by myself, I enjoy my own company, and I'm no longer sure everyone is watching if I decide to go to dinner alone or with a child or another female friend. I enjoy shopping at my leisure and if I feel like really scrubbing up the house I do it. Otherwise it is always clean but not sterile, and the kids and I have learned to throw the covers up on the beds in the morning and each one cleans up after himself. We don't have those big knock-down drag-out battles about dust bunnies and burned-on grease on the cookie sheets and waffle iron, etc. We still have the cleanest house around, the laundry is done, mending, yard work, wood supply in and everything; just not the big fights about the procedures. I feel if the end result is the same, the child or adult should be able to use their own intelligence to accomplish the result. I don't believe every step must be in black and white never changing. . . .

Did you know sudden death does *not* occur if a child wears two different sets of stripes on their sock tops? I just found out after I went to work in May that that promised curse was a lie. Here I am 44 and I was still struggling to get the washer to give back those mates to socks. I thoroughly believed the only way any decent person would wear socks was mated. Lo and behold as I look around at those with crossed legs or kids playing in the yard I find that other people in this world have unmatched socks too—what a surprise! Some of them are even children of non-working mothers.

This courageous woman had made peace with herself. She had learned what to expect of herself in relationships instead of desperately trying to live up to what she imagined was expected of her by others.

Christmas three years later brought another letter from her. There had been other letters in between, one ending with the affirmation of love, "Always your friend and sister in the gospel and

love of Jesus Christ." She had married again, but this time not because of loneliness or insecurity.

> I sure didn't know marriage could be fun and very rewarding. I
> didn't realize husbands can also be your best friend and confidant.
> I didn't realize women had a right to happiness too. Boy, what a
> nice thing to wake up to. . . . I am very grateful for a kind,
> tender, loving husband who is understanding of me and one who
> walks with me; studies with me; travels and vacations with me;
> and generally makes our lives happy. I am grateful to be able to
> return in kind these things to him with a happy, willing, and
> cheerful heart. I am very grateful to our Heavenly Father for all
> the lessons in life he takes the time to teach us. Sometimes I am
> sure it would be easier for God to just put the knowledge and ex-
> perience into our heads than to let circumstances teach us the prin-
> ciples He wants us to learn. We weep and wail all the time we are
> learning! But, in the end, the rewards are always greater than the
> test and we are so much stronger for all the efforts we have made.

This strong, good woman had made a healing transition from
relationships whose troubles extended generations back until their
origins were lost. Her children and grandchildren were being
treated in almost total, loving contrast to what had prevailed in
previous generations.

These three special people whose stories I have recounted, by
learning to love themselves became, in Obadiah's words, as
"saviors . . . come up on mount Zion" (Obadiah 1:21), and freed
their families from generations of wounded and crippled relationships. They were the figures by and through whom a wonderful,
redeeming transition occurred. They accomplished the great healing of which Isaiah spoke:

> And if thou draw out thy soul to the hungry, and satisfy the af-
> flicted soul; then shall thy light rise in obscurity, and thy darkness
> be as the noonday: and the Lord shall guide thee continually, and
> satisfy thy soul in drought, and make fat thy bones: and thou
> shalt be like a watered garden, and like a spring of water, whose
> waters fail not. And they that shall be of thee shall build the old
> waste places: thou shalt raise up the foundations of many genera-
> tions; and thou shalt be called, The repairer of the breach, The re-
> storer of paths to dwell in. (Isaiah 58:10–12.)

Love of God

Who would deny the admonition of John that "if a man say, I love God, and hateth his brother, he is a liar"? (1 John 4:20.)

An older couple had retired to do all those things they had looked forward to. A bishop intervened, who invited them to help Latter-day Saint Vietnamese refugees relocate in the United States. This man and wife spent two years helping these war-ravaged people cope with such challenges as the power company, English as a second language, and their profound homesickness.

This couple acted as had their brothers and sisters of the Church nearly two thousand years ago wherein, as ancient documents tell us, goods and services were rendered to the needy (see Acts 2:44–45; 3:32–35). This was done "according to the discretion of the bishop, [and] it was distributed to support widows and orphans, the lame, the sick, and the aged of the community; to comfort strangers and pilgrims, and to alleviate the misfortunes of prisoners and captives, more especially when their sufferings had been occasioned by their firm attachment to the cause of religion" (Edward Gibbon, *The Decline and Fall of the Roman Empire*, vol. 1 [New York: Modern Library, n. d.], p. 427).

Muggeridge related love of God to the washing of the disciples' feet. "Jesus demonstrated once and for all that the Son of Man was the servant of men; that whatsoever was arrogant, assertive, dogmatic or demagogic belonged to the gospel of power, not to his gospel of love . . . that in abasing themselves, men attain the highest heights, and in glorifying themselves, they sink to the lowest depths." (*Jesus, the Man Who Lives,* pp. 151–52. See copyright and permission information, page 15 herein.)

This kind of love was discovered by a father and mother whose efforts to save their prodigal son eventually required complete submission to their covenants with God as they loved Him by loving an unlovable son. The father wrote for both parents.

I feel to share some of these thoughts with you . . . [and] with others who anguish as we have for almost fifteen years. Looking back, it seems like only yesterday, but when you are struggling through the darkness, each day seems like a year. With all the concern that we have had for Richard, we have come to love and respect our Father in Heaven in the sense that in his wisdom, he will not violate the agency he has given to each of us. How often we would have had it otherwise . . . especially when ours was such a worthy desire . . . the saving of our own son! . . .

As we look back upon our own behavior . . . we can now see areas where we erred. . . . As much as we regret our mistakes, we also realize that every other couple does likewise to lesser or greater extents. . . .

You will recall that in the account of the Lost Sheep the Savior seems to teach us that when One is lost, the Chief Shepherd . . . personally goes after The One in the wilderness.

I was intrigued by the fact that he not only rejoiced when he found it, but 'he *lifted* it up and *layeth* it on his shoulders.' I believe that is indicative of the need for the lamb to feel the warmth of his Master's body wherein is safety. . . .

As we went through some of the bad times with Richard, we learned that we must never give up! Faith, hope, and charity must ever prevail. We had to hope. We had to have faith. We had to have charity! But we had to discipline a boy we had not disciplined properly in earlier years. . . .

I remember well one night when he came for a visit while under the influence of some drug. We learned to look into his eyes; that way we knew if this was our son, or the side whose behavior patterns we couldn't predict well. He was nervous and ill at ease. In this kind of mood it was not unusual for him to go into fits of rage like slamming doors until they would collapse. He finally got up to leave. As he did so, I also got up and walked over to him and said: "Richard, you think you have loyal friends right now; but you don't. Always remember that there are two people and only two who will always love you and will be loyal to you as long as you live. One is your mother. The other is your father. Now as you go out that door, remember that we love you and pray for you." Even while he was in that semi-stupored condition the Spirit touched his soul, because I noticed tears well up in his eyes and the nervousness melted away. He responded: "Thanks, Dad." And slowly and quietly up the stairs he went and was gone. . . .

After the end of summer he asked [his mother] to ask me if he could come back home. I let him know that he would be welcome on condition that he abided by the rules of our home, which included family nights, family prayers, being employed, doing his share of work, attending church meetings with the family, and total compliance with our standards. He agreed to this and kept his word. After about a month, we couldn't believe what we were experiencing. He was really determined to do well! I asked him what it was that had caused the change. He said: "Dad, I have finally learned to think better about myself." It took about another year to straighten out all the kinks.

Through bitter travail these parents transformed themselves from ordinarily good people to loving disciples of Christ. Countless parents struggle to reclaim wayward children. When this arduous task of love is undertaken as a covenant with a loving Father in Heaven and as a Christlike service, strength is received to endure the whole way.

The previous story has a sequel. It was told me by this good father several years later when I sought his permission to publish his experience.

Due to business reverses the father found himself in severe financial difficulty. As is usually the case, he was struggling with the emotions as well as with the legal tasks of such problems. Richard by this time was established in his own business. When he learned of his father's situation he quickly provided financial, organizational, and emotional support. As one can appreciate, as urgent as was material aid, the help his father cherished the most was his son's love and loyalty. The prodigal had not just returned; he now gave healing relief to the father and mother who had wept and prayed for him in years past.

A young woman, not yet married, learned a similar lesson about how to love God as she served a mission among the poorest people in primitive circumstances far from her comfortable home. She used *wood* as a symbol of her self-imposed burdens and *crystal* to symbolize God's burdens on her.

> I would like to share a realization with you all. . . . It's as if up until my decision to listen to the Spirit and [come out here] that I put extra and unnecessary pieces of wood as burdens upon myself. . . .
>
> Now I feel that I'm being taught and guided with patience and love (from a very understanding Heavenly Father) to carry His crystal burdens upon my shoulders. These (*all* God's children) souls are more precious than crystal. . . . He could carry His crys-

tal much easier, but because I have a desire to help Him, He helped me remove my burdensome load of old wood and He's trusting me to carry His crystal (precious experiences with fragile and special people, . . . new understandings of scriptures).

And I realize now that through this service (and *all* service) we can see the different views of life, directions, love, meanings. . . . He lives!

Before now I never realized the real godly promises that come from service! Also the secrets of God, His love, plan, . . . that are revealed *through service* are endless! Endless joy and growth! Endless as He is.

Love, felt for God, neighbor, and self, enriches all relationships. Love defines us, it disciplines us, it enables us to understand ourselves, but only when it is felt and expressed actively. It even ennobles the approach of death, as one Christlike widow testified.

I read your book *Human Intimacy*. As I read the case about the woman whose husband had become impotent, I felt that I could never survive such a situation. Just a few years later I found my husband had prostate cancer, which had spread to the bone marrow. The standard treatment for prostate cancer is to perform an orchiectomy, since prostate cancer feeds on testosterone. Because of that and the pain from the cancer, all sexuality had to cease in our marriage.

My husband lived only fourteen months after the surgery. I went through several months of desperation and tears in having to give up my source of reassurance and affection, knowing of course that I was not being rejected but still feeling the loss of not being "wanted." As my husband's illness progressed, I was able to forget about myself in taking care of his many needs. This included bathing him. The first time it was very hard to run my hands over his body to wash him, and I felt ashamed of myself for my feelings as I saw this once strong and happy person stand in the shower holding onto the towel bar, barely able to support his weak and pathetic body. Eventually he had to be bathed in bed. I had to regard him very differently now. The life of that frail body became all that kept his spirit with me for the short time left.

As I took care of him and his needs, we became closer friends than we had ever been. His needs included diapers the last few months. When I had to clean him this way the first time, he looked into my eyes and simply said, "Thank you." My greatest happiness was just to talk to him. I learned to let him wake me up at any time of the night to talk to me even though I had to go to work each day. I learned to love him more than I ever had before, because now I knew him as my brother in the spirit and as my best friend in mortality. A year ago last month he died.

A mother of four, divorced and struggling with ordinary and some extraordinary challenges, had spent most of her years believing that few people, if any, liked or loved her. Eventually she began to sense the Savior's love for her. Here is just a portion of her rejoicing: "The Savior is carrying this burden for me right now. . . . I want to hear his voice and I want to see Him face to face. I am going to strive for this every day. For the present I am very thankful for this shield that I have. . . . It is very clever of the Lord to help me to understand His love this way. It makes me realize that He does know me and knows what will work."

With the nobility of these examples in our hearts let us conclude our attempt to understand how to enrich or heal relationships. This we will do with the instruction and prayer and blessings of him who personifies the richest love and who heals all despair. We can put mortal relationships in eternal perspective by glimpsing the all-encompassing, never-ending love of the Savior of all mankind, and of the Father of all our spirits.

If ye love me, keep my commandments. . . . Peace I leave with you, my peace I give unto you: not as the world giveth, give I unto you. Let not your heart be troubled, neither let it be afraid. (John 14:15, 27.)

This is my commandment, That ye love one another, as I have loved you. Greater love hath no man than this, that a man lay down his life for his friends. (John 15:12–13.)

Father, I will that they also, whom thou hast given me, be with me where I am; that they may behold my glory, which thou hast given me: for thou lovedst me before the foundation of the world. O righteous Father, the world hath not known thee: but I have known thee, and these have known that thou hast sent me.

And I have declared unto them thy name, and will declare it: that the love wherewith thou hast loved me may be in them, and I in them. (John 17:24–26.)

For God so loved the world, that he gave his only begotten Son, that whosoever believeth in him should not perish, but have everlasting life. For God sent not his Son into the world to condemn the world; but that the world through him might be saved. (John 3:16–17.)

Index